MW01076918

SOCIOLOGY MEETS MEMOIR

Sociology Meets Memoir

An Exploration of Narrative and Method

Margaret K. Nelson

NEW YORK UNIVERSITY PRESS

New York

NEW YORK UNIVERSITY PRESS
New York
www.nyupress.org

Library of Congress Cataloging-in-Publication Data
Names: Nelson, Margaret K., 1944–   author.
Title: Sociology meets memoir : an exploration of narrative and method /
Margaret K. Nelson.
Description: New York : New York University Press, [2024] |
Includes bibliographical references and index.
Identifiers: LCCN 2024008769 (print) | LCCN 2024008770 (ebook) |
ISBN 9781479827312 (hardback) | ISBN 9781479827329 (paperback) |
ISBN 9781479827350 (ebook) | ISBN 9781479827336 (ebook other)
Subjects: LCSH: Sociology—Biographical methods. | Sociology—Study and teaching. |
Sociology—Research. | Biography. | Autobiography.
Classification: LCC HM527 .N45 2024 (print) | LCC HM527 (ebook) |
DDC 301.072—dc23/eng/20240812
LC record available at https://lccn.loc.gov/2024008769
LC ebook record available at https://lccn.loc.gov/2024008770

This book is printed on acid-free paper, and its binding materials are chosen for strength and durability. We strive to use environmentally responsible suppliers and materials to the greatest extent possible in publishing our books.

Manufactured in the United States of America

10 9 8 7 6 5 4 3 2 1

Also available as an ebook

For Robert Zussman

CONTENTS

PREFACE

I have liked reading memoirs for years. But I turned to them seriously several years ago, as part of my sociological practice, for two reasons. I had retired so no longer had the financial support to conduct and transcribe interviews or to hire students to help with the coding. (This was before Zoom turned our world upside down and inside out.) And, if truth be told, I was sick to death of traveling the world just to undergo the stress of conducting interviews. Why not, I thought to myself, as I started a project on family secrets, let the interviews come to me in the form of published writers telling stories they were now ready to reveal.[1] Coincidentally, COVID-19 exploded, leaving us all homebound. That first year was easier than it might have been otherwise had I not curled up with a large pile of good, bad, and mediocre memoirs.

And then at the beginning of the second year of COVID-19 isolation, my husband developed one minor, then a second serious, followed by a third devastating health problem. As I struggled to keep my balance amid medical appointments and profound anxiety, fiction felt too flighty; I just could not enter a world of make-believe. At a different time, or with a different personality, I might have turned to religious texts or poetry. Instead, I devoured memoirs to help me stay grounded. As Diane Bjorklund notes in her study of autobiography, these works "can help us make sense of our lives and give voice to thoughts and feelings that we also may have had." They thus provide, Bjorklund adds, quoting literary theorist J. Hillis Miller, a way to "investigate, perhaps invent, the meaning of human life."[2]

The year before the pandemic, my sister and I had written about the African American woman who took care of us when we were little girls. For the most part, that project focused on Mable Jones and not on us, although to tell her story we had to reveal significant parts of our own.[3] Two years later, we collaborated once more, to write a social history of a progressive Quaker summer camp we had attended as preteens and teens.[4] Again, we had to probe memory and reach out to people we had known as our younger selves. Clearly, I was inching closer to memoir as practice. Yet I had no interest then—and still have no interest now—in writing my own memoir.

Casting about for a project, I challenged Ilene Kalish, my two-time (not two-timing) editor at NYU Press. What should I write about? In her second pass she suggested this: "Well, I did notice that at the [Eastern Sociological Society] conference there were a couple of panels on the sociology of memoir. I took that as a good sign for your book. What about a book for sociologists that would define it, provide examples, and not exactly be a how-to, but maybe a little guidelike? I just think that this could be worth exploring. And it would be short too." This was immediately appealing on both grounds: useful, perhaps, in promoting my forthcoming book *and* short. More importantly, I thought, it would help me understand my own research as well as my naïve fascination with the lives of others.

As is the case for most worthwhile projects, it turned out to be a good deal harder and of greater interest than I had anticipated. I had been intimidated by literary theory as an undergraduate English major. Did I really have to dive into it again? I had left teaching behind once I retired. Did I really have to think about how to excite students? I never especially understood the concept of autoethnography. Did I really have to assess it? Yes, and yes, and yes, and then a lot else.

Ultimately, I found my way through these abstruse topics and even came to enjoy the work (if not always, occasionally). The encouragement and advice of colleagues helped enormously in both ways. These include Emily Abel, Margaret Andersen, Mindy Fried, Mary Tuominen, Maxine

Baca Zinn, Robert Zussman, the anonymous reviewers for NYU, and, of course, Ilene Kalish, who got me started. Special thanks go to Karen Hansen, who not only cheered me on but also read and offered enormously wise comments on my first draft; to Jennifer Pierce, who took time out of a busy day to remind me that this was my book and I could be as selective as I wanted; and to Rebecca Tiger, who told me that she thought the book needed to include a discussion about writing and then sat down and wrote that chapter herself. And finally, as always, I am grateful to Bill Nelson for always being there and for (usually) listening.

Introduction

This book is a guide—not to a city or country or region of the world but to a particular genre of writing, memoir, in which individuals tell stories about some part of their lives and implicitly claim that those stories are "true." And more specifically this book is a guide for readers with a particular focus: both new and experienced sociologists who want to know how they can engage with memoirs as part of their method, practice, teaching, research, and learning.

Why should sociologists be interested in memoirs? As sociologists we frequently use stories as a way to understand how people make sense of themselves and their social worlds.[1] Memoirs have the advantage of being stories people are willing to tell a broad public and not just an individual interviewer.[2] Moreover, unlike interviews, memoirs grant agency to the person telling their story. They provide the "participant" an opportunity to take the lead, to consider their life in depth, and to choose which aspects of that life they want to share with others.

To be sure, memoirs have evoked enormous fury from literary critics who decry their recent prominence; these critics are especially scornful of memoirs written by people considered to be "nobodies." Among those critics, journalist Neil Genzlinger a decade ago wrote with full-throated contempt, "Memoirs have been disgorged by virtually everyone who has ever had cancer, been anorexic, battled depression, lost weight. By anyone who has ever taught an underprivileged child, adopted an underprivileged child or been an underprivileged child. By anyone who was raised in the '60s, '70s or '80s, not to mention the '50s, '40s or '30s."[3] But if literary critics are dismissive, others find unique and robust benefits in the use of memoirs in the social sciences. Historian Emily K. Abel noted that what "literary critics view as problems, many . . . may regard as gifts."[4] That is, although limitations remain in who can—and does—write and then publish a memoir, the memoirs that exist provide access to voices from the past, to voices that have traditionally been marginalized, and to voices that might otherwise be difficult to reach by interviewers even in this modern age of Zoom technology.

Moreover, unlike the materials qualitative sociologists normally use for their research, published memoirs constitute significant social phenomena in their own right. As sociologist Arthur Frank notes, "They affect how others tell their stories, creating the social rhetoric of" what is, in his case, illness.[5] This rhetoric, along with literary conventions, is, ultimately, another source of constraint. But the telling (whether constrained or not) is there for the readers to encounter and evaluate. And given the memoir boom, readers are far more likely to encounter these personal stories than academic sociology. Only in our wildest dreams would as many people read a sociological analysis of drug use as would read Matthew Perry's account of the money he spent to overcome his addiction or Jennette McCurdy's memoir *I'm Glad My Mom Died*, which also exposed addictive behaviors.[6] Only in equally fantastic dreams would as many people read a sociological analysis of personal relationships as would read Gail Caldwell's account of her friendship with Carolyn Knapp in *Let's Take the Long Way Home*.[7]

In short, published memoirs have social significance. They shape how people understand a diverse range of experiences such as living in great wealth, being a ballet dancer, experiencing childhood abuse, or enduring the stigma of stuttering.[8] Historians Patricia Hampl and Elaine Tyler May illustrate this importance with reference to Anne Frank's diary, noting that through publication what is usually thought of as being private enters the public domain. This is how, they write, "a little girl's diary, faithfully kept in the threatened secrecy of her hidden life," came to stand "as the greatest testamentary document to the worst recorded events of the twentieth century."[9]

And memoirs can do even more than narrow the space between private and public. Memoirs not only record and provide testamentary documentation of noteworthy events but also can change or confirm how we think about social norms. Some memoirs, in their very telling, reinforce hegemonic ideas and the narrative frames we apply to social issues. We can think, for example, of J. D. Vance's *Hillbilly Elegy*, which accounts for a person's success (and failure) as produced by individual agency and not structural forces.[10] Other memoirs challenge hegemonic ideals and offer alternative narrative frames. Here we can think, for example, of how frequently in *Between the World and Me* Ta-Nehisi Coates links the personal issues of difference and discrimination faced by African Americans to broad sociopolitical systems that have lasted for centuries.[11] Some memoirs might even provide inspiration for social movements that resist oppressive regimes by introducing entirely new narrative frames. We can recall here, for example, Anne Moody's *Coming of Age in Mississippi* and *The Autobiography of Malcolm X*, both of which educated White and Black people about struggles for civil rights in the United States and thus gave them a new way to think about oppression.[12] That is, memoirs "act" by shaping how people think about and respond to the world around them.

Most of those who pick up this guide will know something about the landscape of memoir, having been there before as readers, teachers, students, or writers. But even experienced travelers can be quickly overwhelmed. Related terms abound—life writing, life narrative, personal narrative, autobiography, personal sociology, private sociology, sociological autobiography, autobiographical sociology, *testimonio*, autoethnography.[13] Controversies also abound. Scholars debate the extent to which context constrains what can be considered an acceptable storyline. They probe the question of what kind of evidence memoirs provide. They explore the reliability of memory. And they consider why we have entered a "confessional age" when anyone and everyone has the audacity to write about their own experiences.[14] These topics have enormous relevance for the theories and methods with which sociologists conduct their work. This guide intends to help sociologists navigate this diffi-cult terminological and theoretical terrain, whether they already know something about the landscape or are encountering it for the first time.[15]

Defining the Field

But what are memoirs, and are they different from other forms of per-sonal narrative like autobiography and testimonio?

Memoirs versus Autobiographies

If you ask Google (or AI) to distinguish between memoir and autobiog-raphy, numerous answers pop up. They all say one version or another of the same thing. Autobiography, we learn, tells the story of someone's life in chronological order, starting with birth and ending at the time of writing (W. E. B. Du Bois was in his nineties when he wrote his last memoir);[16] its promise is to "explain the development of a personality."[17] While considerable craft might go into the writing, the focus is on verifi-able facts. One might look up the records of the subject's birth, marriage, divorce, and remarriage to assess veracity.

By way of contrast, memoirs are usually considerably more limited in "temporal depth and narrative aim," less likely to be an account of an entire life but more often an account of one part of a person's life or one specific experience (which can include a relationship with some other person).[18] They offer an interpretation of a segment of a life, not its en-tirety.[19] Hence, memoirs depict the experience of abuse in childhood (e.g., Dorothy Allison's *Bastard Out of Carolina*), an episode of illness (e.g., Susan Greenhalgh's *Under the Medical Gaze*), or a relationship to a father (e.g., Miriam Toews's *Swing Low: A Life*), to name a few of the many topics.[20]

This characterization makes memoir a subgenre of autobiography and often consigned to a degraded status because anybody can write one, hence the contemptuous term "nobody memoir."[21] Of course anybody can write an autobiography too, but they probably will not because publishers publish and readers read memoirs and autobiographies for quite distinct reasons. We read autobiographies because we are interested in the writer and want to know more about their life; we read memoir because we are interested in the event/issue (e.g., an experience of illness) or the social arena (e.g., life in prison) rather than the individual.[22] On occasion memoirs focus on other people and the author's relationship with them. That is, to make life confusing memoir can, and often does, step into the territory known as biography, as when writers tell the story of a parent, a friend, or a teacher (e.g., Mitch Albom's *Tuesdays with Morrie*).[23]

Memoirs versus Testimonios

If autobiographies relate the lives of "famous people," another genre—testimonio—does something quite different, relating the lives of subaltern people, those who might otherwise not have a voice. Testimonios, which have their origin in Latin America, are formally defined by John Beverley in *A Companion to Latin American Literature and Culture*:

> A *testimonio* is a novel or novella-length narrative, produced in the form of a printed text, told in the first person by a narrator who is also the real protagonist or witness of the events she or he recounts. Its unit of narration is usually a "life" or a significant life experience. Because in many cases the direct narrator is someone who is either functionally illiterate or, if literate, not a professional writer, the production of a *testimonio* generally involves the tape-recording and then the transcription and editing of an oral account by an interlocutor who is a journalist, ethnographer, or literary author.[24]

Not surprisingly, as is the case with memoir and autobiography, the definition changes depending on who is doing the talking or writing. Recently, Norma E. Cantú, a professor at Trinity University, defined testimonio more loosely as she discussed how it was used by the Latina Feminist Group, who gathered essays for *Telling To Live: Latina Feminist Testimonios*.[25] She declared that she, among other Latin American scholars, had thought of testimonio as a "means to tell our stories of survival as Latinas in the United States" and that those who contributed an essay "went beyond the usual format of having a narrator telling a story via an interlocutor" and beyond a focus on a "particular event."[26] Cantú also defined testimonio as a subset of personal narrative but added that "not all personal narratives are testimonios. That is, the testimonio as a first-person narrative is perforce personal; however, the content of the testimonio distinguishes it from a personal narrative where the author merely narrates a first-person story without it necessarily being about survival or endurance." She continued with her argument: "I would go as far as to expand the notion of testimonio as personal narrative to include certain tales or personal narratives of survival. Moreover, there is an element of community in testimonio that is absent in personal narrative. [Rigoberto] Menchú's testimonio . . . is not just about her own struggle but of the Indigenous peoples of Guatemala."[27] In the same piece, Cantú's co-author, Domino Renee Perez, professor at the University of Texas at Austin, largely agreed with this definition but added a more political element: "With testimonio, there is an urgency and intentionality to it that can incite change or bring awareness to systemic conditions and/or issues. Personal narrative does not have those obligations, a feature that represents a key division between personal experience narratives and testimonios. Whether in long or short form, testimonio is told to effect change in the present, even when it is about the past."[28]

Two scholars at San Jose State University, Kathryn Blackmer Reyes and Julia E. Curry Rodríguez, similarly argued that testimonios—unlike other forms of personal narrative—necessarily present a call to action: "What is certain is that testimonio is not meant to be hidden, made intimate, nor kept secret. The objective of the testimonio is to bring to light a wrong, a point of view, or an urgent call for action. Thus, in this manner, the testimonio is different from the qualitative method of in-depth interviewing, oral history narration, prose, or spoken word. The testimonio is intentional and political."[29]

In short, while testimonio and memoir are both genres that involve personal narrative and storytelling, the two have emerged in distinct cultural contexts and have distinct characteristics. Testimonio originated in Latin America and is strongly associated with social and political movements, especially in countries with histories of oppression. In those countries testimonio is a form of resistance, a way for otherwise voiceless people to speak both of their own experiences and of the experiences of other members of a community. A narrator might dictate a testimonio to someone else; the narrator might also tell the story themself. Memoirs can come from individuals of any cultural background who relate some portion of their life experience. While they might also involve editing by a ghostwriter, the presumed voice is that of the author.[30] And although memoir writers might choose to tell a story with political import, the genre does not require that element.

No Ideal Types but Limits

As with any attempt to create an ideal type or draw a sharp distinction among genres, reality gets in the way. This is especially the case with memoirs because memoir writers negotiate between available models or methods and their own writing style.[31] But there are other issues beyond the difficulty of separating one genre from another. One piece of reality is that these days memoir sells, and many genres of personal storytelling, regardless of how autobiographical or testimonial they might be, are now referred to as memoir.[32] So although Michelle Obama writes her life story from birth to the "present," and although we as readers probably pick it up because we are interested in her (who wouldn't be, given that it's Michelle Obama), her book is widely advertised as a memoir.[33] But we're interested in Michelle Obama not least because she can tell us about a relationship with and inside stories about Barack Obama and because we are curious about just what happens inside the White

House. Hence her book is both memoir and autobiography and a bit of biography too.

And to make life more confusing, some "memoirs" cross boundaries in yet other ways. Sociologists Barbara Laslett and Barrie Thorne viewed this blurring as an advantage when the sociologists who contributed to their collection of essays *Feminist Sociology: Life Histories of a Movement* merged personal narratives and social theory.[34] Outside of sociology, the blurring exists as well. Daniel Mendelsohn's beautiful book, *An Odyssey: A Father, a Son, and an Epic*, is described on the back cover as follows: "By turns family memoir, brilliant literary criticism, and a narrative of education."[35] And if that isn't enough, the blurb continues, "Most of all *An Odyssey* is a love story." A recent bestseller, Lucas Bessire's *Running Out*, combines family history, a contemporary search for understanding, and a critique of water policy that, the author must hope, will produce political action.[36] Another recent memoir, Annette Gordon-Reed's *On Juneteenth*, is described as "weaving together American history, dramatic family chronicle, and searing episodes of memoir."[37] By its title, Denise Chávez's book, *A Taco Testimony: Meditations on Family, Food and Culture*, suggests the genre of testimonio. But the Amazon description calls it a "a warm and exuberant memoir, with recipes," and in a review Alyssa Revels also calls it a memoir, adding that it "references the genre of *testimonios*."[38]

My focus in this guide is memoir (and not autobiography or testimonio), but I occasionally use the other genres to make a point.[39] The memoirs included here are primarily freestanding, book-length manuscripts. However, in some cases (especially in chapter 3) I draw on short (chapter-length) pieces. Although memoirs today can take the form of blogs, I include only those published in book form, and I concentrate on those memoirs that take a traditional written form rather than relying on graphic representations.[40]

And except for essays written by sociologists about their lives, I refer to material that has *not* been collected or analyzed for the purpose of another project. Although memoir writers do not have free rein (but must fit their stories within conventional frames to be accepted for publication), already existing collections of essays are likely to be guided by the persons organizing them.[41] One final limitation: Many social scientists include the "I" in their writing. In long methodological statements they explain their position, biases, impediments to researching a particular topic, language choice, and other vital issues that alert the reader to their understanding that they are not objective reporters telling a single truth. Sociologists also frequently use their own experiences to enhance the narrative quality of their study. In *Weaving a Family*, Barbara Katz Rothman, for example, identifies herself as having had relevant experiences that led to and deepened her research; in telling these stories, she makes herself more authoritative and creates a more interesting analysis.[42] Lynn Davidman's *Motherloss* intertwines her own narrative about the loss of her mother at age thirteen with the voices of sixty other people who experienced a similar loss.[43] And, to take another example, Jesse Daniels, in *Nice White Ladies*, acknowledges that she, too, is White and was reared to be "nice."[44] But this guide focuses on books that make the personal experience *primary*. Therefore, despite their contribution to literature, books such as Rothman's, Davidman's and Daniels's do not appear here. Admittedly, however, as I explain further when I discuss autoethnography, the line between using the "I" to spice up one's writing and making the "I" the focus of the writing is a pretty blurred one.

Audience and Organization

After years of teaching and conducting research as a professor in a small liberal arts college, I initially viewed this guide as a resource for people like me: sociologists interested in using memoirs in the classroom, in their research, or as part of their own sociological practice. But the more I worked with the relevant materials, the more I realized that I too was learning, that I too was a student of these issues. For the most part, then, I do not distinguish between teacher and student but address sociologists (and social scientists) in general, whether they have been in the discipline for years as I have been or are just getting their first delicious taste of it. However, I do address a more specialized audience in the fourth part of this book, in chapter 7, where I delve into debates about autoethnography, and in chapter 8, where guest author Rebecca Tiger offers advice to colleagues teaching sociology.

I divide the chapters in this guide into four approaches to the broader topic. Part I provides a brief overview of historical issues relevant to sociologists interested in memoirs and addresses the broad questions of who writes memoirs, what shapes the writing, and what we expect from those writers by way of truthfulness. Part II asks what we might learn about becoming and being sociologists through the autobiographical essays and memoirs of those in the discipline. Part III explores specific uses of memoir for sociologists as a tool for learning sociology and as a way of collecting evidence. In part IV, addressed to scholars, I raise issues about memoir writing as method and practice.

More specifically, in chapter 1 I consider arguments about the causes of the contemporary memoir "boom." Many of these explanations echo what we learn is the literary critics' contempt for the boom itself. But other explanations not only laud the boom but find within it evidence of democratization and a new form of citizenship.[45] And some scholars in the latter group note the ways in which memoirs represent the declaration of a generation protesting received wisdom and ready to listen to new voices and new ideas.[46] Doubts about "objective truth" that gave rise to the subjectivity of memoirs resemble doubts by social scientists in the second half of the twentieth century that gave rise to new theoretical and methodological approaches. I conclude this chapter by discussing the "narrative turn" in social science and placing memoirs within this context.

I discuss the issue of the complexity of the "self" who writes a memoir in chapter 2. I also introduce the notion of constraints on that writing itself as part of the understanding of how we can interpret any given memoir or set of memoirs on related topics. The frequency of, and the attention paid to, what have been called "hoaxes" remind us that we expect some form of honesty from memoir writers. I ask what we expect memoir writers to be honest about.

In chapter 3, the first chapter in part II, I incorporate both full-length memoirs and a greater number of short essays written to describe how sociologists have explained their fascination with the discipline, the origin of their own conceptual apparatus, and the shape of their careers. In a complementary chapter, I narrow my perspective to explore how three sociologists—W. E. B. Du Bois, William H. Whyte, and Renée Fox—used their autobiographical writing as a moment to reflect on and evaluate one of their first pieces of independent sociological research. These reflections reveal elements of the backstory of research: time limits, impediments, confusions, and mistakes. They also expose pride and resistance to critique. And they raise the question of what standards are most appropriate for the evaluation of research conducted under different critical regimes.

In chapter 5, the first of part III, I consider how memoirs can help us develop our sociological imaginations. I explore a different use of memoirs by sociologists in chapter 6. I describe in detail four examples of sociological writings in which the authors used memoirs as their primary data and consider the range of issues that arise in using memoirs in this way. I begin part IV by examining the ways sociologists have used personal experience as the basis for their studies, focusing on what is known as "autoethnography." I consider how this approach contributes to debates about sociological methods. In the last chapter Rebecca Tiger also discusses issues regarding the use of personal writing as a way for both new and advanced sociologists to develop their own sociological insights.[47]

One of the reasons memoirs and sociology bump into each other is because, at their best, they both illuminate the sociocultural influences that shape individual lives. In my conclusion, I raise issues of the similarities between sociology and memoir as well as review some fundamental differences.

PART I

Conceptual Issues

1

The Memoir Boom and the Narrative Turn

Starting at the turn of the twenty-first century, critics noting the new prominence of memoirs in the literary firmament began to write about what was then called (and continues to be called) the "memoir boom." Ben Yagoda, professor of journalism and English at the University of Delaware, in his simply titled book *Memoir: A History*, traces this phenomenon to the early 1990s.[1] He argues that during an empathetic era, spurred by "Bill Clinton's feel for pain" and "Oprah Winfrey's furrowed brow and concerned nod," memoirs had begun to be one of the most common forms of nonfiction available to readers.[2] According to his data, the popularity of this form had continued unabated: "Total sales in the categories of Personal Memoirs, Childhood Memoirs, and Parental Memoirs increased more than 400 percent between 2004 and 2008."[3] Moreover, memoirs had become far more than simply popular: "Memoir," Yagoda insists, had "become the central form of the culture: Not only the way stories are told, but the way arguments are put forth, products and properties marketed, ideas floated, acts justified, reputations constructed or salvaged."[4]

In *Boom! Manufacturing Memoir for the Popular Market*, Julie Rak, professor of English and film studies at the University of Alberta, provides a later date for the "memoir boom," referring to "a period roughly spanning the first decade of the twenty-first century."[5] But she also sees no sign of its abating. And Thomas Couser, now professor emeritus of English at Hofstra University, in his *Memoir: An Introduction*, offers additional evidence, of its continued popularity, noting that among its fifteen hardcover nonfiction bestsellers, the November 21, 2010, issue of the *New York Times Book Review* listed seven memoirs. He adds that among the *Book Review*'s "twenty paperback nonfiction bestsellers, eleven can be classified as memoirs."[6]

Explaining the Memoir Boom
A Selfish Society Full of Nobodies

The elements of this boom quickly ran into harsh criticism in the public press. Some directed their vitriol especially at memoirs by fleeting celebrities and relatively or completely unknown people. In 2002, journalist Lorraine Adams wondered whether "the nobody memoir is merely methadone to keep us from the smack of Sally Jesse Raphael."[7] Almost a decade later, a staff editor at the *New York Times*, Neil Genzlinger, wrote far more contemptuously, describing the few authors "who would be memoir-eligible under the old rules . . . lost in a sea of people you've never heard of, writing uninterestingly about the unexceptional, apparently not realizing how commonplace their little wrinkle is or how many other people have already written about it."[8]

Many of the scholarly explanations for the memoir boom echo the literary critics' and journalists' contempt for the new spate of memoirs and especially for the emergence of the "nobody memoir." Some argue that the genre achieved its popularity because of "the well-worn culture of 'me,' given 'an expansive new currency by the infamous baby boomers who can think of nothing else.'"[9] Equally disdainfully, others argued that the memoir boom could be explained by writers responding to some of the worst traits of our society, including "more narcissism overall, less concern for privacy, a strong interest in victimhood," a therapeutic culture, and the "growth of Alcoholics Anonymous and the recovery movement," which turned the "terrible, terrible things" that happened to people into something that could sell.[10] Others joined in, referring to a reading public who uncritically gobble up whatever nonsense publishers publish, bookstores sell, and readers buy (and then maybe—or maybe not—read). In this way critics characterize our interest in understanding the lives of other people as deriving from some essential lack in our-selves.[11] Still others, with a slightly more social scientific bent, explain our interest through the dynamics of capitalism. In this analysis, the memoir boom represents a simple ruse by publishers to get more people to buy more books by appealing to what some call our "base" instincts.[12]

Questioning Authority

We could, however, look at the memoir boom from another perspec-tive, thinking of it not as the last gasp of self-obsessed people living in a selfish society but as a new way for people to challenge the status quo and reject received wisdom. Thomas Larson, author of *The Mem-oir and the Memoirist: Reading and Writing Personal Narrative*, dates the memoir boom to events following 9/11 "when it became difficult for Americans to make sense of what authorities told them."[13] From this perspective, memoir can be seen as a dissenting voice against pro-paganda, a radical substitute of the voice of individual experience for that of experts. Along these lines, some theorists argue that this dis-senting voice emerged from the baby boom generation as it matured, challenging putative authorities ("don't trust anyone over thirty") and struggling to speak in its own voice.

Mary Karr, writer of her own well-known and very moving mem-oir, *The Liars' Club: A Memoir*, as well as a book addressed to memoir writers, speaking to an interviewer from *Salon* in 1997, added another point of view.[14] She insisted that toward the end of the twentieth century people had rejected traditional authorities and now wanted "some sort of moral compass" and that the subjective could supply that "because all of the measures of how we are doing—the church, community life, religious or government leaders, certain kinds of values, family—no longer mean what they once did." Some twenty-five years later, writing in the *New Yorker* to celebrate French memoir writer Annie Ernaux's Nobel Prize, critic Adam Gopnik similarly linked our love of memoir to our "need for verifiable, or at least credible, personal history" at a "time when so much else seems constructed and untrustworthy."[15] Fenton Johnson, author of a memoir about growing up gay in the 1950s, refers to Anne Frank as an example of how memoir can satisfy the social need for a way to preserve our shared history without relying on the esoteric or abstruse voices of authority.[16] Patricia Hampl and Elaine Tyler May concur when they argue that rather than listening to storytellers, we now read published memoirs so that we can connect to, and understand, our past: "Millions more readers worldwide know the poignant story of Anne Frank's life in hiding than know the facts of Hitler's rise to power. A successful memoir is not a product of the self-obsession of a selfish, me-first generation; it is evidence of literate people's recognition that the written word has replaced the story told by the winter fire as our means of establishing and preserving cultural memory."[17]

Lift Every Voice

Still other scholars (and some of them are precisely the same people who show contempt for the memoir as a dominant genre) locate the rise of the memoir as evidence of a new era of radical democratization. They insist that memoir is a democratic form because its sources derive from the ways in which ordinary people speak about their lives—with spontaneity, through anecdotes, and in stories passed down through generations. Couser, for example, argues that "the point here is not to elevate memoir as a genre (above its sibling genre, the novel) nor to disparage it as non- or sub-literary, but merely to point out what seems a defining and significant distinction. Precisely because it does not have to take written form, life narrative is deeply rooted in daily life; therein lies a source of its vitality and significance when it does take written form, as in the contemporary memoir." He continues, "To put it slightly differently, memoir has unique democratic potential because, being rooted in these everyday practices, it is more available to amateurs than other genres."[18]

In short, rather than bemoaning the fact that now anybody can write a memoir, we might celebrate this phenomenon as one that allows access to voices previously marginalized, and this is a significant reason sociologists might well be advised to learn from it. Now, with the rise of the "nobody" memoir, we hear from women who were previously silenced, from members of marginalized communities, from those with disabilities, and from those who were formerly voiceless (e.g., those with Down syndrome, autism, Alzheimer's).[19] Along these lines, historian Elaine Tyler May writes that "the study of history came to embrace the lives and feelings of those previously ignored by historians: ordinary people, not those who have already made their mark."[20]

Of course, people might still read memoirs for voyeuristic reasons. But as they do, they simultaneously and perhaps inadvertently help create community. Matt Becker, whose essay is included in the Hampl and May collection, argues that even if occasionally memoir appears to be a "gratuitous celebration of the self [and thus] yet another example of individualism trampling community," the subjectivity of memoir can help "generate feelings of human connection." He explains more fully,

> Indeed, because these self-explorations [in memoirs] are grounded in the details of an author's lived experience, they tend to have greater depth than personal stories on TV, greater truth than relationships from social networking sites. As a result, memoir has the potential to produce in us a strong connection to the author's humanity, and it is from this connection that the genre also has the potential to build community. . . . If memoir can promote these common interests through a focus on individual uniqueness, then its celebration of the self is not gratuitous. It instead has a vital purpose.[21]

Fenton Johnson makes a similar point when he writes that "paradoxically it is through subjectivity that one best gains access to truth, the enduring, timeless wisdom that enables us to have and keep faith in ourselves and in each other, in our collective capacity to live in harmony with each other and with our planet."[22]

Moreover, memoir reading not only might help build community but also, especially when reading those written by nobodies, might confirm and then reconfirm the rights of anyone to become a celebrity, of any private person to "act on a public stage."[23] Julie Rak believes this form of democratization is a particularly American phenomenon. She writes that because the United States is "built on the ideal of democracy and the practice of political representation," it is there that memoir has become "one of the technologies for the private self that can be shared." She continues, linking reading and writing memoirs to acts of citizenship and to the possibility of engagement in movements for social change: "[Memoir] becomes a way for readers to think publicly, but from the private sphere. It creates the possibility of social movement through personal movement. In this sense, memoir as a genre has the potential to create social action."[24]

Rather than viewing the memoir boom as a distinctly American phenomenon, Jill Ker Conway, onetime president of Smith College and author of several memoirs, starting with the account of her childhood in Australia, *The Road from Coorain*, views the memoir boom as a global event.[25] Only partially tongue in cheek, she asks, "Why is autobiography the most popular form of fiction for modern readers? Why are so many people moved to write their life stories today? And what is it about the genre that makes it appeal to readers not just in the Western world, but also in non-Western cultures, like those of Japan and India or the many cultures of Africa?" In answering her own rhetorical questions, Conway points to the increasing abstruseness within the disciplines of literary criticism, philosophy, history, and psychology for which memoir provides a cure by tackling in accessible language the important questions "about what it means to be human, how the individual is shaped by society, whether she or he ever has free will, what shapes the imagination, what talents are valued and what misunderstood, how great political figures are formed and how they resonate with their followers."[26]

Down with Objectivity

Conway is not alone in linking the memoir boom to simultaneous developments in academic disciplines. Other scholars also believe that doubts about those developments made room for more reliance on individual ways of knowing and moral relativism.[27] Among those scholars, Yagoda argues that the subjectivity of the memoir dovetails with the "doubt or denial of 'objective truth' that gathered force throughout the twentieth century." He references the growing use of the "I" in fields like history and anthropology, those moments when scholars began openly acknowledging that they were simply individuals making claims rather than objective and neutral authorities disseminating what would previously have passed as "truth." Ultimately, Yagoda reminds us, some scholars have written memoirs rather than relying on formal disciplinary notions about distance (and he cites here Henry Louis Gates Jr.'s memoir *Colored People*) as did others who termed their research autoethnography rather than ethnography, placing themselves in the center of observation and analysis.[28]

In short, it makes sense to view the memoir boom as one aspect of a broader methodological movement that urged scholars to interrogate their own biases as they went around choosing their subject matter and then gathering and analyzing their data. That is, much as scholars in several fields began to look at how the subjects of their research constructed the stories revealed to their questioners, scholars also began to look at the ways in which they themselves, as the people focusing on specific issues and then conducting the research and writing the results, also mattered. In addition, other changes in the world of social science—and in sociology itself—had an impact.

What Is the Narrative Turn, and Why Did It Happen?

Starting in about the 1980s sociologists along with other social scientists began to speak of a "narrative turn" in their disciplines. By this they meant, most simply, an outpouring of scholarly work based on personal narrative evidence—that is, on "retrospective first-person accounts of individual lives."[29] Helpfully, discussions of the "narrative turn" begin by defining narrative. In an early discussion, sociologists Patricia Ewick and Susan Silbey write that to "qualify as a narrative" a particular communication must have three elements:

> First, a narrative relies on some form of selective appropriation of past events and characters. Second, within a narrative the events must be temporally ordered. This quality of narrative requires that the selected events be presented with a beginning, a middle, and an end. Third, the events and characters must be related to one another and to some overarching structure, often in the context of an opposition or struggle. This feature of narrativity has been variously referred to as the "relationality of parts" or, simply, "emplotment." The temporal and structural ordering ensure both "narrative closure" and "narrative causality": in other words, a statement about how and why the recounted events occurred.[30]

Others make similar claims for narrative, emphasizing the same sets of elements in essentially the same order. Leslie Irvine, Jennifer Pierce, and Robert Zussman, in the introduction to their collection of essays on narrative sociology, for example, focus on sequence, a narrator who tells the story, the "organization of events in some relationship to one another," selectivity (a narrator does not report *all* events), and linkages (or plot) that give the events meaning.[31]

Drawing on these definitions, we can think of the "narrative turn" as a way of describing that "moment" when narrative entered—or, some argue, reentered—sociology.[32] Irvine, Pierce, and Zussman distinguish between two aspects of that turn. First, narrative became a way of "doing sociology . . . a means of exposition and explanation." That is, sociologists began to rely on a narrative style in their writing and chose to explain the sequence of events with respect to that narrative. As further explanation, these three scholars illustrate their ideas with specific examples: Diane Vaughan's analysis of the *Challenger* launch decision, Mitchell Duneier's *Sidewalk*, and Alice Goffman's *On the Run*.[33] These narratives, they argue (and many would concur), have made sociology more interesting and even something that people can read like a story. Because they avoid jargon, works like these are accessible to those who are not experts in the field. (Not surprisingly, when these kinds of analyses are used in the classroom, students often refer to them as "novels.")

Second, sociologists began to interrogate the use to which diverse kinds of narratives were put in different contexts."[34] Or, as Ewick and Silbey put it, narrative also became something to explain, the "object of inquiry and explanation," as sociologists began to explore how people "construct and communicate their understandings of the world." Some sociologists—and here is where the narrative turn links to the memoir boom—focused on the narratives themselves and began to draw on collections of narratives (e.g., interviews, oral histories, accounts) to make sense of something of sociological interest. Again, an example offered by Irvine et al. helps: medical sociologist Arthur Frank explores the different voices through which people with serious illnesses explain their experiences (in a book I discuss extensively below).[35]

Much as the memoir boom can be explained in a variety of ways, so too can the narrative turn in the social sciences. As has been implied already, these explanations include an interest in making sense of how people understand themselves and an interest in hearing voices that had been marginalized. But in making that turn sociologists were interested not just in letting new voices speak but also in approaching those voices through new critical traditions (Marxism, feminism, subaltern theory, queer theory), which, Maynes, Pierce, and Laslett contend, began to "question the epistemological foundations of positivist social science, recognize the historical and social specificity of all viewpoints and subjectivities, and emphasize the perspectivity intrinsic to knowledge production."[36] As sociologists from these traditions actively challenged the hold quantitative studies and its claims to objectivity had on the field, they substituted qualitative approaches for quantitative ones and reflexive accounts of the role of the researcher for the notion of an objective but invisible "I."

And it was not just criticism of older approaches that inspired and propelled the narrative turn. Scholars made profound claims for the new methods. For example, Barbara Laslett and Barrie Thorne, in their introduction to a collection of essays written by the first generation of feminist sociologists, argue that the life histories they collected could "bring forth 'experience' and 'voice'"; they could "link the personal and the political, the private and the public."[37] One special and especially useful feature of this form of narrative that Laslett and Thorne note is the focus on the details of historical context and the influence of context on social action. Another is the focus on the dimension of time and moments of transition. A third is the frequent interrogation of the ways social scientists have overlooked the significant meaning individuals place on their actions by narrowly talking about personal "interests." In short, these two editors claim that life histories, stemming from the individual, can provide the basis for more general knowledge and for building theory. And according to Laslett and Thorne they can also "illuminate the dual aspects of experience as event, happening, occasion, and as subjectivity and interpretation."[38] Similarly, Ann Goetting, in her essay introducing a different set of essays, notes that the personal essay "fills knowledge gaps" by providing "privileged strategic information on human interaction and social structures."[39] She adds that as a second advantage this form is "a tool for interpreting the intersection of the micro and macro levels of the social order."[40]

Not surprisingly, many early, mostly White, feminists found life writing to be a vehicle for introducing women's voices and perspectives and for the analysis of gender as an organizing principle of social life. Women of color added the analysis of race as being of equal significance; many stressed the importance of taking an intersectional approach when seeking to understand lived experiences.[41] In their more personal writings, scholars like Patricia Hill Collins sought to challenge and correct the historical marginalization and exclusion of the voices of Black women.[42] Others also began to speak. Gay men and lesbian women told "coming-out" stories and, in so doing, revealed the effects of homophobia and heteronormativity on their lives.[43] In much of this work the action of telling stories exposed oppression for the writer as well as the audience. That is, the writing itself became an "illuminating experience."[44] The writers claimed agency, presenting themselves as people who could tell their own stories rather than submit to the stories told about them.

Also, not surprisingly, counterclaims emerged. Gillian Whitlock, for example, reminds us to ask questions about what we are reading: "Which bodies are breathed into life, and which lives are being brought into view by autobiography? Do life narratives circulating via modern technologies facilitate social justice and thinking about sovereignty, community, and subjectivity across cultures? If life narratives exert transformative agency—as they have on behalf of subordinated peoples in the past—in whose interests and to what ends, [do they do this] at the present time?"[45] In raising these questions, writers like Whitlock acknowledge the social importance of memoirs, the ways in which they can be both inclusive *and* exclusive, liberating *and* controlling.

Taken as a whole, then, scholars have made bold claims for narratives. They have argued that narratives can "operate as a form of social control," especially when they embodied social norms. In this vein, we could think about fairy tales and how they repeatedly conveyed the idea that personal happiness depended on passivity and beauty for girls and bravery and quick wit for boys. At the same time, scholars argued that narratives can offer multiple truths rather than a single, "objective" truth and that narratives can be subversive. They thus have made both epistemological and political claims for narratives.[46]

Moreover, as noted in the introduction, narratives stand apart from academic writings and have their own importance in the world. But to understand *how* narratives—and, more particularly, the specific group of narratives known as memoirs—have significant effects, we must interrogate them, asking about the self who writes them, the sources and constraints on the stories within them, and the relationship between the story and some verifiable facts or events.

2

Self, Story, and Veracity

In the previous chapter I suggested that memoirs can be viewed as representative of a retreat into the private or subjective when we do not trust the public statements that purport to be objective, as a form of self-aggrandizement, or as evidence of democratization. From a different angle, they can be viewed as a subset of a kind of life writing and, within that, a subset of both biography and autobiography. But they are not only or just any of those things.

Years ago, when I was struggling to describe how people enacted "fictive kinship," a colleague suggested I ask not what the phrase "like a member of the family" *meant* but what it *did* to, or within, a relationship. Guided by this wisdom, I apply something of the same perspective to memoir and ask what it is that it does that other forms of writing (and even other kinds of first-person stories) do not. Regardless of boom mentality and postmodern doubts about objective social science, what do memoirs do to and for us?

A partial answer is that memoirs invite us to think about a "self" in the social world. In this way they almost by definition (and very quickly) excite the sociological imagination: whether consciously or not, memoir writers tell stories that link their "personal troubles" to "public issues." As such they make claims (which they put forward as based on verifiable facts) about how individuals like themselves navigate the world. Justin Snyder, in a review of Thomas DeGloma's *Seeing the Light: The Social Logic of Personal Discovery*, makes much the same point when he writes, "Stories about 'personal troubles,' as well as personal blessings, even when the key protagonist is the self, define 'public issues' or 'shared cultural realities'. . . . Autobiography is sociological imagination."[1] And autobiographies (and memoirs) achieve that sociological imagination when a self (the narrator) tells a story that purports to be, in some sense, "true." In what follows, I examine issues that arise in the consideration of each of these elements: the self who tells the story, the story itself, and the issue of veracity.

What Is the "Self" of Memoir?

Literary critic Thomas Couser tells us that he likes memoirs not because they provide access to or "knowingness about the world out there" but because they provide "knowingness about the world in there: self-awareness, insight into the author's identity, that of some other actual person, or the relation between the two."[2] Memoirs, he argues, offer a "kind of wisdom, understanding of the formation of the self, the nature of one's identity—or of a significant other." But we might ask, who is the self who speaks in memoirs? And how are we, as readers, to discern among the many possible selves?

We can approach these questions first by considering the relationship between the author and the text itself and then also by considering the "types" of selves available to the author. Both issues are recognized by literary critics Sidonie Smith and Julia Watson, who complicate the autobiographical "I" by dissecting it into four separate voices.[3] First, they refer to the "real" or historical "I"—or what they call the "flesh and blood person," knowledge of which is available in places like census records. That self can be verified by readers interested in assessing at least some elements of the narrative. Indeed, as will be discussed further below, writing stories about themselves that included details that could not be verified has gotten some famous people into some very hot water.

Second, Smith and Watson refer to the narrating "I," by which they mean that the narrator draws on some—but clearly not all—of the historical "I's" experiences. Here Smith and Watson recognize that memoir writers are selective both by conscious choice and, less consciously, by the vagaries of memory. That is, memoir writers might opt to—and probably can—narrate only part of their life story. Although all autobiographers will be selective, memoir writers are especially so when they confine their narratives to specific moments (e.g., their childhood) or specific experiences (e.g., an episode of illness). Moreover, whatever gets narrated will be filtered through memory as it is shaped by one's life experiences and personal attributes. That is, while some moments in their lives might be especially vivid, others will be less so and even entirely unavailable to memoir writers. As readers, we might want to think about how conscious we are of writers' selectivity and of the possibility that they can, in fact, remember what they say they do.

But beyond deciding which parts of their experiences to narrate (after unearthing them), Smith and Watson refer to the narrated "I," which they describe as "the version of the self that the narrating 'I' chooses to constitute through recollection for the reader." Thus, they suggest that memoir writers will want to present only some aspects of themselves or will want to present themselves to their readers in a particular light, to curate images of who they are now and who they were in the past. They might, for example, decide to write about those moments when they were kind and generous, omitting evidence of those moments when they were cruel and miserly. Or, in a more confessional mode, they might do quite the reverse. In any case, no one, whether a memoir writer or not, tells anyone else everything; everyone creates the self that they take out in public to show to the world. As a result, as Alice Kaplan, author of the memoir *French Lessons*, writes, "A memoir can never achieve a total truthfulness, in part because [authors] have to decide which part of [themselves] to narrate."[4] And again, as readers we might take with a grain (or teaspoon) of salt some of the assertions any given writer makes about themself.

Finally, Smith and Watson recognize that not all selves can, or will, be presented at any given historical moment. Hence, they write about the ideological "I," by which they mean "the concept of personhood culturally available to the narrator when he tells the story." I will say more about this below when I turn to the issue of the story itself. And I will develop this issue again in chapter 6, where I introduce both Diane Bjorklund's argument that the kind of moral "self" an individual could present has changed over time and Arthur Frank's claims about the possible vocabularies of illness in postmodern times.[5] Each study suggests that the concept of personhood any writer can draw on will be determined by the society in which that writer lives. Therefore, as literary critic and sociologist Paul John Eakin recommends, we should read autobiography "in the spirit of a cultural anthropologist, *asking what such texts can teach us about the ways in which individuals in a particular culture experience their sense of being 'I.'*"[6]

Eakin takes this kind of analysis one step further when he argues that for much of Western history the only model of the self available to an autobiographer was "emphatically individualistic, featuring a 'separate and unique selfhood.'"[7] He notes also that in the relatively recent past this model came under criticism by feminists (among others), who argued that female selves were less individuated than male selves and that their life stories were less linear. Therefore, he concluded, women's autobiographies would be different from those of men. These differences could be considered as sets of binaries: the self presented in women's autobiographies would be more collective (understanding the significance of the private backdrop for one's achievements) than individualistic (or claiming agency), would be more relational (referencing family and friends) than autonomous (standing alone in the world), and would tell its story in nonlinear, discontinuous, non-teleological forms rather than as straightforward, plot-driven narratives.[8]

These binaries help describe some of the differences between the memoirs of men and those of women who write about their careers as sociologists, as discussed further in chapter 3. White men have written about their achievements as the almost inevitable consequence of their individual efforts; their careers follow a plotline that begins with an often casual, occasionally accidental interest in sociology and ends with well-earned recognition and success. White women have written about interruptions and impediments to their careers and about the invisibility of their private lives in public spaces. And both men and women as representatives of marginalized groups recognize the dynamics of power and privilege in the academy as constraints on individual action.

Fruitful as Smith and Watson's four-part dissection of the autobiographical "I" is for thinking about memoir, it implicitly assumes that some stable (even "authentic") self stands behind the narrator as they pick and choose (within constraints) which parts of that stable self to record. But it does not explain the source of that "self." For that, we might turn again to the writings of Eakin, who (along with other social theorists) stresses both what he calls the "substratum of somatic experience," the ways in which "our lives in and as bodies profoundly shape our sense of identity," and, importantly, those "social sources" that produce a self through interaction with, and in relation to, others—including not only other people but also the full set of norms and values that constitute our social worlds.

Moreover, thinking about a relational self opens the possibility not just that there is one self but that we are "multiform creatures," with different selves in different interactions and at different points in time.[9] And one of those interactions, taking place over a period of time, is with one's own former self. As narrative psychologists like Jerome Bruner argue, it is through "self narration"—that is, through the stories we tell about, and to, ourselves—that a "self" emerges.[10] As anyone who has written in any kind of autobiographical vein is well aware, a self is *created* through writing as it is through other types of autobiographical acts.[11] Writing a memoir, like other occasions of self-narration, helps individuals learn what is important, what they care about, what they want to share with others. From this perspective, it is not surprising that Barbara Laslett and Barrie Thorne report that when they asked women sociologists to write their life histories, many of those women found it to be an "illuminating experience."[12]

Reading memoirs as sociologists, we must ask questions about where the authors, themselves, as flesh and blood people stand in relation to the story they tell. How would we know whether they are providing us with accurate information? How do the vagaries of memory shape what they are telling? How selective are they being—and to what end? How might they have changed after telling their stories? And how does that evolution, in turn, shape what gets written?

The Story and Its Constraints

As has been implied by now, the narrator is not in full control of the story; at the very least, the narration will be shaped by what is possible to say at any given time. Recall that sociologists Patricia Ewick and Susan Silbey believe that stories can have political significance, bringing about social change.[13] But they do not grant narratives complete autonomy or the capacity to be written in any way the author might want. Rather, as do others, they tell us that stories "are always told within particular historical, institutional, and interactional contexts that shape their telling, its meanings and effects." Similarly, Maynes, Pierce, and Laslett, when writing about memoirs as a particular subset of personal narratives, remind us that they emerge within specific social, cultural, and historical settings.[14]

Among these settings are literary conventions that influence how people write about themselves: "Autobiographers typically write their life stories within the framework of one or more general plotlines drawn from among the limited number of plausible ones available in circulation."[15] Among the available plotlines, or "patterns for presenting processes of self-knowing," are the *Bildungsroman*, "or narrative of social development," the *Künstlerroman*, or narrative of artistic growth, the confession, the conversion narrative, the testimonio, the quest for lost identity or a lost homeland or family, and the escape to freedom.[16] The differences among some of these, Couser suggests, "are best understood as matters of the underlying relation in each between [two of the many possible] I's"—the "I-now (the narrator) and the I-then (the narrator's earlier self)."[17] For example, in a confession, the "I-now" tells about, and perhaps atones for, deviant or destructive actions the "I-then" took in the past; in a conversion narrative, the "I-now" explains how they have shed what they now believe are the mistaken beliefs of the "I-then." We might also want to ask questions about what can—and cannot—be mentioned at a given point in time. To take one example, many people condemned (and many people praised) Kathryn Harrison's *The Kiss* for admitting to passionate sexual love between a father and daughter.[18]

The reader who identifies the plotline (sometimes from the title itself) knows what to expect: a "quest for a lost family" will end with reunion or, in some cases, the creation of a new kind of kinship; the "escape to freedom" will end with a new life in a less oppressive country or region. Whatever the plotline, the authors themselves might make the links between the former "I" and the present one explicit. Martha Hodes does as much in *My Hijacking*, where she writes about the dramatic events of a summer day when she was at the cusp of adolescence: "I wanted to connect the twelve-year-old girl who buried as much as she could to the grown-up struggling to understand what happened to that girl."[19]

Another constraint emerges from the world of publishing itself. As has been noted already, the memoir boom has broadened the characteristics of the lives considered to be of interest to others. Publishers have learned that readers do not want to hear exclusively from White male "celebrities, politicians, business figures and sports stars."[20] Whatever biases remain in the world of publishing, the voices of marginalized groups now achieve prominence. To take a recent example, in September 2022 the *New York Times* published a list of fifteen recommended memoirs and biographies.[21] Only four of the twelve memoirs were written by White men: the others were written by a Latino male, a gay working-class immigrant from Ghana, a White Canadian woman, an American Asian man, a transgender woman, the daughter of a Swiss Mennonite and a Somali Muslim, an African American woman, and a South Korean woman.[22] Only one of the three biographies was about a White man.

When we mine memoirs for their sociological insights, we need to ask questions about how the context in which they are written constrains the narratives. We might then ask, if there are multiple selves and multiple constraints on what has been written, how do we assess veracity?

Let Us Talk about What Passes for Truth

It has long been argued that fiction can transport the reader to new worlds and create a capacity for empathy. So can memoirs. In Hodes's memoir we learn what it was like to be the victim of a hijacking while traveling with her sister from Israel as a young girl;[23] in *Thinning Blood*, by Leah Myers, we glean insight into the life of a woman caught between White and Native worlds;[24] and in Lucy Grealy's *Autobiography of a Face*, we become painfully familiar with how disfigurement and surgery shape a life.[25] These are reasons why memoirs can incite the sociological imagination and can be useful sources of data for the analysis of sociological issues.

But there is a crucial difference between fiction and memoir in the claims they make and therefore, one would hope, in how we read them. The memoir genre claims to tell the story of "real, not imagined individuals" even if those individuals are constantly changing or, one might say, have multiple selves. Like autobiography, memoir makes a certain "identity claim" that we do not find in fiction: "The author, the narrator, and the protagonist share the same name and vital statistics (such as date of birth). They are identical, in more than one sense: (1) they are all the same person, and (2) their congruence establishes the identity of the memoirist. This is in itself a sufficient signal that a narrative is a memoir."[26] And rather than fantasy, memoir must refer to some "extra-textual" facts like the names of one's parents, the town in which one spent one's childhood, the schools one attended, and the first job one held.

Because we know what genre we have in our hands (or on our screens), we read memoirs and fiction differently. When we read fiction, we suspend disbelief: we willingly and often happily enter an imaginary world. We relish the escape fiction offers. When we understand something to be a memoir (or autobiography) and not a novel (or other form of fiction), we read with different expectations and have different experiences. That is, when we read memoirs, we bring with us an expectation that the author is telling us about something they believe is real. We use our capacity for empathy and identification to put ourselves in the author's place; we read between the lines to make linkages that the author might not make explicit.

Of course, the writer may acknowledge—or we may assume—that the story being told is as the writer remembered it. And from our own experience, we know that memory can be faulty and, as discussed above, will certainly be selective. By calling something a "memoir" the writer explicitly acknowledges the role of that unreliable and selective faculty of memory. Even so, as sociologist Ann Goetting argues, even if memory is in some sense "faulty" and "experience itself is mediated by the ways we describe and interpret it to other," memoir represents its own attempt to arrive at some kind of "truth": "The truth of autobiography is in the *interpretation* of life processes."[27] That is, memoirs tell us not what happened but how writers remember, interpret, and make sense of the events in their lives. And if we identify with or develop empathy with the author so that it "feels" true to us, we might ask to what extent it matters whether the particulars can be verified.

The writer might also acknowledge—or we may assume—that the presentation depends on artfulness and novelistic techniques including selecting some moments in a life and the rearrangement of sequencing of events to create dramatic import.[28] But too much selectivity and too much rearranging can get authors into trouble. As readers we impose limits (of which we might not even be aware) on the unreliability and selectivity of memory *and* on the use of artfulness and novelistic techniques. We feel betrayed when we learn that the author has taken too much license, moved too far beyond what could be cross-referenced to an actual event. And these betrayals are especially significant when the memoir delves into issues of social importance and has a significant impact in the world.

Couser refers to this imposition of limits as a kind of "ethics." He argues that in writing about their lives memoirists "assume two distinct kinds of responsibilities: first, to the biographical and historical record; second, to people they collaborate with or represent in their memoirs."[29] With respect to the first, the memoir writer need not be totally constrained: not everything has to be verifiable. After all, a memoir *is* a work of art. But memoirists (like autobiographers) will be held to what Maynes, Pierce, and Laslett say is the "provocatively" called "autobiographical pact," outlined in 1975 by French critic Philippe Lejeune. Lejeune suggested that a pact existed between the writer and the reader—not in any sense of law but in a sense of convention, implicit understanding, or promise:[30]

> I of course became aware of the fact that autobiography could not merely be defined by its form (a narrative) or by its content (a life), for fiction could imitate both, but by an act, which made it utterly different from fiction, and that act is the commitment of a real person to speak of himself or herself truthfully. This is what I called the "autobiographical pact." . . . An autobiography is not a text in which one speaks the truth about oneself, but a text in which a real person says that he or she is speaking the truth about himself or herself.[31]

Author Fenton Johnson, makes a similar point about the implicit understanding between author and reader implied by the label "memoir": "In writing memoir only a hack makes it up. In writing memoir the rule of the game—the discipline that provides the vessel for memoirists' words—is our contract with the reader that our writing is as truthful to memory as we are capable of being and that we will let the reader know, directly or by implication, how reliable we feel ourselves to be."[32] Johnson takes his argument one step further, noting that "the great memoirists do not conceal their uncertainties." Rather, he adds, they "use them as another tool for making art. They work both from empirically, historically verifiable fact and from the art of constructing and handing the best of all possible stories." For Johnson, then, truthfulness "lies . . . neither in head nor heart alone but in the understanding that these are integrally intertwined and cannot be separated without doing violence to both."[33]

Three contestations around the veracity of memoirs are famous because challengers argued that the authors "transgressed" the "autobiographical pact" in very public ways about very significant issues. James Frey's "memoir," *A Million Little Pieces*, recounting his addiction and recovery, burst onto the literary scene in 2003 and was two years later promoted by Oprah on her talk show.[34] With that endorsement the book quickly rose to the top of the *New York Times* bestseller list, where it remained for fifteen weeks. A year later allegations emerged from the Smoking Gun website that Frey had exaggerated key elements of his story. After initially standing by her man when he was interviewed on *Larry King Live*, Oprah denounced him in 2006, a public humiliation for Frey. Five years later she apologized for not having been compassionate enough in her reaction. Among the many people who have commented about this episode, Julie Rak is especially thoughtful in her argument that the timing of the "moral panic" that accompanied the revelations about the book's veracity coincided with growing mistrust of what George W. Bush had told Americans about the necessity for war in Iraq.[35] Doubts about the honesty of the stories of weapons of mass destruction that had been fed to the American public were conjoined with doubts about the honesty of a best-selling story of overcoming addiction.[36]

But there was more. Not only had Frey played with the facts, but he had taken liberties with a story that Americans care about a lot—recovery from substance abuse. They want an authentic story of redemption through rehabilitation. They might not have felt so cheated were the story about something of less social import, but at this time and in this place they cared. As Daniel Mendelsohn observes, "If the anguish and the suffering aren't real, there's nothing to redeem, and the whole exercise becomes pointless. It is precisely the redemption memoir's status as a witness to real life that makes the outrage so loud when a memoir is falsified."[37]

Another celebrity, Greg Mortenson experienced the same round of celebration followed by scandal. In his best-selling memoir, *Three Cups of Tea: One Man's Mission to Promote Peace—One School at a Time*, Mortenson recounts how after he failed to scale K2, local villagers rescued him and nursed him back to health.[38] In return he promised to come back and build a school in their village. His subsequent efforts to create a charity that established schools for local children brought him tremendous praise and sizable donations. But in 2011 a report on *60 Minutes* alleged that his initial account of how he ended up in the village could not be verified, that some of the promised schools had never opened, and that he had misspent the funds. Author Jon Krakauer, who had initially supported Mortenson's efforts, wrote a scathing denunciation titled *Three Cups of Deceit*.[39] Like Frey, Mortenson had toyed with something Americans cared about, including honest philanthropy and meaningful humanitarian endeavors.

Perhaps the most important story of a challenge to the veracity of a memoir is that addressed to Rigoberta Menchú's *I, Rigoberta Menchú*. The book itself was widely hailed as a powerful story of how Guatemalan peasants had been treated by an oppressive regime; for her work on behalf of her people, Menchú herself was awarded the Nobel Peace Prize in 1992. Six years later Middlebury College anthropologist David Stoll wrote a book that listed discrepancies between Menchú's account of specific events and what he had learned about those same events from his interviews over the course of ten years.[40] To take just one example, Stoll pointed out that although Menchú said that she witnessed her brother's murder, he believed she could not have been there and that her depiction of the event is that of another murder she had witnessed. Subsequently, Stoll himself was challenged by Greg Grandin, who wrote in *Who Is Rigoberta Menchú?* that the Truth Commission in Guatemala was able to substantiate many of Menchú's claims.[41]

Two kinds of backlash ensued after the publication of Stoll's book. Many, and especially those on the political right, used Stoll's story as evidence that Menchú's story was propaganda on the part of the Guatemala Army of the Poor and that those (and especially those on the left) who had bought that story and heralded her had been duped. But many, and especially those on the left, excoriated Stoll, arguing that his book gave space for conservative arguments about the source of political repression and the reaction to that repression in a manner that cast the blame for violence in the region on activists like Menchú and her father rather than on the structural forces that produced that activism.

Other critics of Stoll argued not only that he had taken her story out of context but that he had applied the wrong criteria to his judgment of her story. Menchú, her defenders insisted, was writing testimonio, a specific genre with a distinct set of "truth" claims. These claims are announced in the opening of the book:

> My name is Rigoberta Menchú. I am twenty three years old. This is my testimony. I didn't learn it from a book and I didn't learn it alone. I'd like to stress that it's not only my life, it's also the testimony of my people. It's hard for me to remember everything that's happened to me in my life since there have been many very bad times but, yes, moments of joy as well. The important thing is that what has happened to me has happened to many other people too: My story is the story of all poor Guatemalans. My personal experience is the reality of a whole people.[42]

The firestorms accompanying these three examples illustrate well the demand for veracity and the degree to which a reading public is willing or unwilling to extend its limits. Frey's defense that his story was merely exaggerated had little purchase in an era when so many people were concerned with the vital question (accompanying a war) of whether politicians were lying. Mortenson had an even more challenging time defending his deceptions because he had misappropriated funds. The defense of Menchú succeeded in some quarters not because it argued for the veracity of what she had said but because it shifted the grounds of truthfulness to that represented in a testimonio, even as Stoll's account fueled a conservative response to the events in Guatemala.

From a sociological perspective, we could also argue that Frey and Mortenson did something different from Menchú. Frey's memoir not only told a story about something the reading public cared about but also in its very telling reconfirmed a hegemonic narrative frame. That is, from a sociological perspective, one of the things memoirs do is tell us how to understand social problems. The narrative frame surrounding the social problem of addiction, to which Frey's memoir seemed to adhere, asserted that people get addicted, go through terrible times, hit rock bottom, find a way out through treatment and self-help efforts, and move on to a better life. When it was discovered that Frey had stretched the truth, the frame itself was thrown into question: maybe people do not hit rock bottom; maybe treatment does not work; maybe some addicts never move on. Because the frame itself had such power over the public imagination, rather than rejecting the frame, Frey's audience rejected him. To do otherwise would have raised fundamental questions about the nature of addiction and its treatment. Similarly, Mortenson himself had to be condemned so that the American public could continue to believe in individual philanthropy.

Menchú's account of the suffering of Indigenous people at the hands of an oppressive regime operated on a different level. Rather than reconfirming a preexisting narrative of widespread contemporary significance, it introduced readers to a world and a style of storytelling with which they were unlikely to be familiar. It suggested a way people in the United States might think about, and make sense of, ongoing oppression in Central America. And in doing so it inspired a social movement. Perhaps because her sympathetic readers were less likely to have a handy narrative frame with which to interpret her story but were caught up in the movement itself, they were more accepting of an alternative way to read it and hence to remain loyal to her.

In recent years, some cultural/social critics have claimed that memoirs in general, and not just those considered "fraudulent," have had a central role in what has been called "truth decay," defined by Jennifer Kavanagh and Michael Rich in a book with that title as "increasing disagreement about facts, a blurring of the line between opinion and fact, an increase in the relative volume of opinion compared with fact, and lowered trust in formerly respected sources of factual information."[43] Memoirs, these critics argue, are implicated because they give authority to "personal experience" and personal feeling rather than "facts." We come to believe what someone tells us is true for them, rather than what a presumably more objective reporter states to be the sequence of events in a given situation. Former *New York Times* book review critic Michiko Kakutani takes the occasional defense of both Frey and Menchú as evidence that readers no longer care about the distinction between fact and fiction.[44] The response of those readers, he writes, is "a symptom of just how comfortable people had become with the blurred lines of truth."[45]

In response critics Katherine Mack and Jonathan Alexander would argue that we should not either simply accept or simply reject the claims made in memoirs but rather read differently, not for fact or fiction but for understanding the rhetoric involved when memoirs (and they focus on *Hillbilly Elegy* by Vance and *Between the World and Me* by Coates) make broad social and political claims by drawing on personal experience.[46] More generally, we might ask ourselves just what it is we expect memoirs to tell a truth about as well as how we expect them to tell it.

The three challenges to veracity and the accompanying concerns about truth decay discussed here all have to do with the memoir writers' representation of something that they experienced, saw, did, or felt. But Couser reminds us that memoir writers also have significant ethical responsibilities to respect the "rights and interests of others." Because memoirs refer to "real" people and might even elaborate at length about those people (especially when memoir shades into biography), lives are exposed. Unsuspecting family members, friends, acquaintances, teachers, coworkers, bosses all might find themselves depicted in someone else's story. Memoir writers must constantly make decisions about what matters more—their story and their right to tell it or the right to privacy of the people who populate that story. Occasionally memoir writers will give pseudonyms or acknowledge changing the details of individuals' lives. For example, Sarah Valentine prefaces her memoir, *When I Was White*, which tells the story of not knowing that her biological father was African American during her childhood, with this statement: "Memory is imperfect, and I have truthfully portrayed the events and conversations described in the book to the best of my recollection. I recognize that others' memories of these events and conversations may differ from my own. To that end, some names and personal details have been changed or omitted to protect the identities of those portrayed in the book."[47]

Fern Kupfer, writing about caring for her disabled child Zachariah, makes a similar disclaimer: "For the sake of privacy and clarity, some characters in this book have been fictionalized and some names and places have been changed."[48] But of course, as Dena Davis, a bioethicist, points out, changing the details of a person's life to protect anonymity necessarily compromises some aspects of the truth.[49] Names, physical characteristics, the places we lived and worked—they also determine who we are and why we are what we are.[50]

Drawing on these ideas about the futility of demanding "truth" in memoirs, Jane Ribbens, lecturer at the Open University, suggests we might not want to approach a memoir "with ideas about its 'objectivity' at all, but instead explore what it can tell us about our own 'subjectivities.'" From this point of view, she argues, "the factual validity of the autobiography is not even relevant since it is to be regarded as providing insights into the subjective perspective of an 'individual.'"[51] Ultimately I would disagree, at least for some uses of memoir in sociology. If sociologists are going to rely on memoirs to inspire the sociological imagination—or as evidence about issues of social importance—we need to depend on their accurate representation of the connections, or links, they make between the individual and the society in which that individual lives. Of course, we might simply enjoy the story for how it helps inform our own subjectivities. But then we are no longer reading memoirs as sociologists at all.

PART II

Sociological Memoirs

3

Becoming and Being

Have more sociologists than scholars in other fields engaged in the practice of memoir writing as a way of explaining their reasons for studying their discipline, their conceptual apparatus, or their careers? Perhaps there is no way of knowing. But it seems likely that sociologists would be especially equipped to accomplish that task. Robert K. Merton, an early functionalist, suggested as much some years ago: "The autobiographer has the advantage of being the ultimate Insider [and] the biographer has the counterpart advantage of more readily being the distanced Outsider." By way of contrast, he added, because of their training sociologists stand in a unique position, being able to combine "the complementary advantages of both Insider and Outsider while minimizing the disadvantages of each."[1]

Some scholars have worried that too few of their colleagues have taken advantage of that positioning. In 1988, in his introductory essay to a collection of chapter-length autobiographies by sociologists, Merton noted that a sizable number of influential figures—Marx, Durkheim, Weber, Simmel, W. I. Thomas, and Talcott Parsons—were among those who had left no such account.[2] Robert Zussman, a retired sociologist and good friend, made a similar point in a 1996 review of several autobiographical books.[3]

Merton and Zussman together list the autobiographies of Charles Page, George Homans, Reinhard Bendix, Don Martindale, Herbert Spencer, Lester Ward, Pitirim Sorokin, Robert McIver, William Whyte, Norbert Elias, and Paul Feyerabend.[4] Since Merton and Zussman made their lists, we can add quite a few other book-length memoirs by sociologists, including Renée Fox, Peter Berger, Pierre van den Berghe, Amitai Etzioni, George Henderson, and Stephen Turner.[5] We can also add W. E. B. Du Bois (mentioned by neither Merton nor Zussman), a sociologist who left behind not just one but three separate autobiographies.[6] And finally, we can add the memoirs of a couple of contemporary sociologists—Victor Corona and Donna Gaines[7]—and the sets of linked essays of Tressie McMillan Cottom and Victoria Reyes.[8] All but four (Fox, Gaines, Cottom, Reyes) are men; Henderson, Du Bois, Ryes, Cottom, and Corona stand out as the writers who do not identify as White.

Because of the narrowness of the population of sociologists writing book-length memoirs, in this chapter I draw also from short autobiographical pieces. Many sociologists have written this type of essay in conjunction with a special occasion or life event such as a retirement,[9] as part of the responsibility of holding a position in a professional organization,[10] as a preface or postscript (or both) to another piece of scholarship,[11] or for some unstated reasons of their own.[12] Still many other sociologists have written personal reflections in response to an invitation to contribute to an edited collection. I include three collections of essays by what the editors considered "prominent" sociologists,[13] several collections of the experiences of women sociologists,[14] and three collections focused on issues facing scholars of race and ethnicity.[15] Finally, I include a number of recent collections of essays exploring the academic careers of members of marginalized communities and more specifically the writings of the sociologists within them.[16]

In what follows I explore how these individuals account for why they became sociologists, the origins of their central ideas, and the nature of their careers; I also reflect on how some of these experiences differ by the characteristics of the sociologists themselves and on how these experiences have changed over time. And I argue that by reading and analyzing these memoirs we can better understand what it means to learn and practice sociology itself. That is, by using the lens of other people's memoirs, we can evaluate our own experiences in our discipline.

Becoming

Accidental Entry

Some themes run through the many different accounts of becoming a sociologist. Especially prominent is the notion that sociology is an intellectual activity that one stumbles into. In the words of quite a few, it is an "accident."

Not surprisingly, stumbling into sociology was especially common among earlier generations. As Peter L. Stein explains (in the conclusion to a collection of essays from sociologists who had retired from teaching), people are more likely to grow up with aspirations to be doctors, lawyers, entrepreneurs, or entertainers than grow up dreaming of sociology.[17] Among the early stumblers, Peter Berger, author of *Invitation to Sociology* and *The Social Construction of Reality*, describes his entry into sociology as "accidental" because, as an immigrant, he enrolled in courses with that title hoping they would teach him about American society.[18] Beth Hess, author of numerous books on aging and social gerontology, found the demeanor of the government department at Rutgers less congenial than that of the sociology department, where they would accept an application from a woman who had deferred higher education while raising children.[19] In her homeland of China, Min Zhou, whose work has focused on immigrant life and ethnic assimilation among Asian Americans, learned about sociology when working as an interpreter for some visiting sociologists. She writes that her career had circumstantial origins: "In some sense, I didn't really choose sociology: opportunity came my way by chance. If I had happened to be an interpreter for anthropologists, I might have been drawn to anthropology instead."[20] Earl Babbie, whose *Practice of Social Research* has shaped how scores of students approach methods, admitted that his sociological career was the result of the simple vagary of course scheduling: "So I think I looked around for courses at pleasing times. You know, 10:00 in the morning or something like that. I ended up in the course on Cultural

Anthropology taught by Doug Oliver. I have to tell you, I just sat there the entire semester. My head must have been spinning. I had never thought about the things that he was talking about, the kinds of cultural differences of human beings. And you could study that. That could be your job. You could study that."[21]

The Enchantment of Sociology

Accidental exposure or not, as Babbie suggests those who become sociologists—eventually if not immediately—find enchantment in what the field has to offer, often because sociology introduces them to concepts that mesh well with their orientation to the world. This is as true for those who contributed to the discipline generations ago as it is for those who have made their mark in the quite recent past.

Dennis Wrong, an early critic of the limits of structural functionalism, writes that "[sociology] seemed relevant to my socialist beliefs." He was far from being alone in hoping that sociology would be an appropriate home from which to change the world.[22] In the conclusion to a collection of "sociological autobiographies," Charles Vert Willie notes that quite a few sociologists (and he lists here Hubert Blalock, Rosabeth Moss Kanter, Theda Skocpol, Lewis Coser, and William J. Wilson) "may be classified as ethical moralists who want a better world and hope sociology can help them achieve this goal."[23] More recently, introducing the autobiographical essays of fifteen contemporary scholars whose writings have changed our understanding of race, Margaret Andersen and Maxine Baca Zinn write that quite a few "began their careers working in antipoverty projects, equal-opportunity and job-training programs, or immigrants' rights organizations [and that] many also participated in the movement activities of the 1960s and early 1970s—Freedom Summer, the Farm Workers' Strike, and other campus-based activist actions." "Social activism," these editors conclude, "fueled . . . interest and commitment to sociology *because* of sociology's perspective on structural inequality."[24]

Sociology attracts others because it helps them make sense of significant aspects of their lives. Jessie Bernard, an early feminist scholar, describes being intrigued by the subject matter but acknowledges that it was "a long time before I recognized why sociology was so fascinating to me, how much history I was myself a product of and participant in."[25] The particular experience of having been (or still being) an outsider draws many to the field.[26] Fred L. Pincus, who taught for over four decades at the University of Maryland, and Peter M. Hall, who spent much of his career at the University of Missouri–Columbia, were both what has been called "red diaper babies," children whose parents' commitment to communism made them "different" from their peers and fearful that that difference would be detected.[27] As the only Jew in his community, David R. Simon, the author of nine books, including *Elite Deviance*, had his own experience of being an outsider: "I was forced to sing Christmas carols in school and to listen to New Testament readings by one of my teachers. These early life experiences created a deep sense of alienation and being on the outside looking in to the dominant culture."[28]

Adia Harvey Wingfield, now a professor of sociology at Washington University in Saint Louis and the 116th president of the American Sociological Association, believes that her race and class, in her words, "meant that I was mostly accepted but was still attuned to the ways I was different." She further explains the effects of difference: "I spent a lot of my youth and adolescence trying to understand this paradox of almost fitting in and observing just how and where race made me different. I knew that I wanted to understand these sorts of questions, and after an 11th grade sociology class, realized that this was the academic discipline that could provide the tools for this undertaking. Sociology could give me the framework to understand how and why race mattered, generally speaking, and hopefully could offer the tools to think through a path to a more equitable society."[29] Victor Corona, whose family moved from Mexico City to the wealthy suburbs of Westchester County in New York State, writes similarly about "growing up between categories" and how that meant that he "never had a sturdy identity to define" him. He explains how this positioning drew him to sociology: "And so I've spent most of my life in search of [an identity]. It's no surprise that I ended up in a profession where it's my job to study other people's identities. This null sense of self makes me really curious about people's mannerisms and lingo in certain settings, the ease and flourishes with which some speak."[30]

Depending on the circumstances, one's gender, race, ethnicity, sexual orientation, political affiliations, religion, ability, and social class can produce powerful feelings of marginality, of being on the outside; they can thus arouse a curiosity to which sociology can respond in helpful and interesting ways. But some people feel "different" simply because of their personalities, interests, or experiences. These feelings also draw people to sociology. For example, Donna Gaines, author of *A Misfit's Manifesto*, writes with glee about how learning sociology at Kingsborough Community College enabled her to put labels on her childhood and adolescence: "Tricks of the trade, tools of craft, sociological concepts clarified so many things. . . . I had felt like a vapor for most of my life, and even this was explained. In fact, vast bodies of knowledge addressed it. It was called *alienation*."[31] Moreover, Gaines adds, sociology not only offered her a way to understand how she had been (and remained) a "misfit" but also saved her life: "If the existential truth of life's essential sadness hits you too soon, you may never learn how to walk through it. You'll spend years stumbling alone in the valley of fear. . . . The lucky few found a distraction, a temporary reprieve. For some, it was their music, for others, it was their kids. For me it was sociology."[32]

The Origin of One's Ideas

Gaines was lucky because sociology helped her find her place in the world. Other sociologists, no matter the reason they were attracted to the field, did not initially believe that sociology resolved their issues or fulfilled its promise of enchantment. Some floundered before finding their footing. Jeffrey Olick, professor at the University of Virginia, was already studying sociology when he had an "intellectual push" from what he calls "the wave of so-called 'turns' in the social sciences of the 1980s—linguistic, narrative and cultural." This intellectual energy came together with his personal interest when he "read about the German historians' dispute of 1985–86, in which public intellectuals debated how appropriate it was to place memory of the National Socialist past at the center of German politics and identity." As a secular Jew about to marry a non-Jewish German woman, he was drawn, "obviously" he adds, to historical issues. When the intellectual and the personal came together, Olick found, in his words, "exhilaration . . . being at the start of a field of study of 'collective memory.'"[33]

Years earlier, Lewis Coser, author of *The Functions of Social Conflict*, recalled being uneasy with the Parsonian "bias in favor of equilibrium, balance, common values and harmonious adjustment"; ultimately his own experiences (in French concentration camps and in Marxist sects) required him to free himself from that bias and to focus on discord.[34] A generation later his teaching helped his student, Donna Gaines, find her way within sociology as he "lifted [her] up from the gutters of positivism," enabling her to leave "the material world" and enter "the spiritual realm."[35] As Coser and Gaines imply, even those attracted by sociology sometimes had moments of disenchantment, moments of feeling as if the field did not reflect *their* experiences. Fortunately for their heirs, some of these theorists drew on their unease to re-create the discipline.

One of these re-creators is Dorothy Smith, the author of the ground-breaking *Everyday World as Problematic*. Smith struggled for years with her awareness that the world she "encountered every day and night in the ordinary ways [she] went about it, didn't seem to be present in sociology" and that "the realities of people's daily lives were beyond anything sociology could speak of." And although she wanted to "fix it," initially she "didn't know how."[36] Eventually Smith used this unease to refashion sociology from a feminist perspective. Indeed, for many women—of her generation and subsequent ones—feminism made the difference, not in turning them into sociologists but in enabling them to make sense of the sociology they were already studying, saving them from disenchantment, and providing the impetus to create new forms of social thought. Bernard writes dramatically about this process: "After the dark night of the 1940s and 1950s the renaissance of feminism in the 1960s was like a burst of beautiful lights that illuminated the scene and brought with it a spreading warmth."[37] Joan Acker, a leading analyst of gender and class, writes that before feminism, she always felt "like an outsider" in sociology, afraid that she just couldn't "get it." Once she began to develop into a feminist sociologist (and she credits the work of Dorothy Smith, among other influences), she began to ask questions that made sense to her, "not questions dredged from some 'body of literature' and couched in the concepts of some bodiless 'theorist.'"[38] Ultimately, she learned that she had to "get the man out of [her] head," and she titled her essay after that insight.

Moments of disenchantment and recovery are especially prominent among scholars from racially marginalized communities. Elizabeth Higginbotham, a founding member of the Center for Research on Women at the University of Memphis, reports that "as an outsider" she "saw social inequality differently from the structural functionalism in texts in the 1960s" but that it was some years before she, along with her collaborators, invented ways to think differently about race.[39] Like Higginbotham, Nina Johnson, associate professor at Swarthmore College, implies that "an experience of inequality and the desire to make sense of it" can not only draw African American sociologists to the discipline but also provide the impetus to "explain the social world, to make it legible, to make sense of and interpret their experiences and to do the work of making the invisible visible."[40]

In the introduction to their edited volume, Andersen and Zinn make a similar point about the impact of "moments of racial awakening" on scholars who pioneered studies of race and ethnicity: "'Feeling race,' even in early childhood, fostered the sociological awareness these scholars now have" as they drew on their experiences to develop their ideas.[41] Among those included in their collection, Michael Omi, co-author of *Racial Formation in the United States*, writes that he had "attended three very different schools—one predominantly Black, one overwhelmingly Asian, and one largely White," and that "these experiences profoundly shaped [his] understanding of what race is, the social meanings we impart to it, and how race is both structured and lived."[42] Pierrette Hondagneu-Sotelo, author of *Domestica: Immigrant Workers Cleaning and Caring in the Shadows of Affluence*, also explains how her background inspired her sociology:

> My mother was the live-in domestic worker, and my father, the gardener, when they met at a house in Woodside, California. So many themes in my research derive, in some way, from these life histories, including how migration is gendered; how, for women, a gendered struggle plays out within patriarchal families and communities; the unexpected reconstructions and reformulations of gender practices and norms that come about through migration and settlement; the importance of social networks in migration and settlement and the uneven ways resources are shared, and the informal and unarticulated rules governing jobs like domestic work and the social organization of *jardinería* landscape maintenance.

Summing it up, she muses about her upbringing, "Who could have cooked up a better recipe for feeling like an outsider?" Ultimately, she insists, a stance like hers is a prerequisite for good analysis: "All sociologists need to be a little inside and a little outside, peering into social worlds without fully belonging."[43] Sociologists like these changed the field, moving and stirring subsequent generations. Wingfield, for example, writes that one of the "very first books" she read for an under-graduate course "was by a sociologist named Patricia Hill Collins. It was called *Black Feminist Thought*." And, she adds, "It is not an exaggeration to say that that book blew my mind. Collins offers a formidable critique of the very discipline of sociology."[44]

When inventive scholars could not modify the discipline they some-times moved beyond its confines and joined other departments. Frus-trated with sociology's inability to consider central work that integrated "the perspectives of women and people of color," Evelyn Nakano Glenn, whose first book was *Issei, Nisei, War Bride: Three Generations of Japa-nese American Women in Domestic Service*, ultimately found her way to "Ethnic Studies and Women's Studies Departments."[45] Writing a genera-tion later, Victoria Ryes explains that still today she finds that sociology neither promotes the contributions of important scholars of the past nor fully supports those with a broad orientation and that interdisciplinary departments remain necessary:

> My own field of sociology, for example, tends to not teach or include the historic contributions of Anna Julia Cooper and Ida B. Wells-Barnett alongside those of Marx, Weber, or Durkheim. Nor teach or include the contemporary brilliance of Kimberlé Crenshaw and Gloria Anzaldúa, for example. After over a century since his first book, *The Philadelphia Negro*, was published, W. E. B. Du Bois is only now beginning to be recognized and incorporated into mainstream and elite sociology. . . . The types of scholars who are hired at top institutions and receive the most funding, and the types of scholarship that are published in the top journals in the field, still reflect a sociology that is exclusionary. Indeed, it was these ex-clusions that led to the necessary emergence of interdisciplinary fields and departments, such as Ethnic Studies, African American / Black Stud-ies, Asian American Studies, Latinx Studies, Native American Indian / Indigenous Studies, and Women and Gender Studies.[46]

Careers

Many memoir-like pieces—whether full-length books or short essays—are testaments to the inspiration of a special professor, a unique department, or an unusual institutional energy at a particular point in time. And many scholars acknowledge that they relied on supportive mentors and groups of collaborators to launch and then sustain their careers.

Inspirations

Among the foundational thinkers who mention inspiring teachers, Peter Berger traced his interest in sociology to the influence of three professors at the New School for Social Research—Albert Salomon, Alfred Schutz, and Carl Mayer—who introduced him to the key ideas of Weber and Durkheim and, through Schutz, to the question that stuck in his (and Luckmann's) mind. The question went "something like this: If the sociology of knowledge is going to be true to its name, it will have to deal with everything that passes for knowledge in everyday life."[47] At Harvard, Earl Babbie found his intellectual excitement in courses taught by Talcott Parsons, as did Renée Fox.[48]

Of course, not everyone was motivated by the same person. Scholars exhilarated some individuals and failed utterly with others. Reinhard Bendix, who brought comparative-historical studies to U.S. sociology, lauds two University of Chicago professors—Louis Wirth and David Riesman.[49] Illustrating the particularity of inspiration, another Chicago student, William H. Whyte, author of Street Corner Society, offers a significant critique of Wirth and Blumer but great praise for W. Lloyd Warner and Everett Hughes.[50]

Among scholars studying gender, Marjorie DeVault, author of Feeding the Family, acknowledges the enormous influence of Dorothy Smith, who visited Northeastern while DeVault was a graduate student there.[51] In At the Heart of Work and Family: Engaging the *ideas of Arlie Hochschild*, Karen Hansen and Anita Ilta Garey collected essays by nineteen different scholars (including themselves) who grounded their scholarships in Hochschild's concepts.[52] Jennifer Pierce, who studies racialized and gendered inequality in American workplaces, named the considerable influence of Arlie Hochschild as well as Nancy Chodorow, Nancy Scheper-Hughes, Tomás Almaguer, Robert Bellah, Michael Burawoy, and Eli Sagan.[53] A generation later, Wendy Leo Moore mentions Jennifer Pierce as being an important influence on her life.[54] Among those studying issues of race and ethnicity, Enobong Hannah Branch, of Rutgers University, lists courses by Dr. Karyn Loscocco and Dr. Hayward Derrick Horton; Margaret Andersen, author of *Getting Smart about Race: An American Conversation*, cites the important influence of William Julius Wilson, Louis Killian, and Michael Lewis, three men who "opened [her] eyes to a structural analysis of racial inequality."[55]

Sometimes these influences were indirect, through publications rather than through face-to-face encounters. I have already noted how Wingfield acknowledges the importance of Patricia Hill Collins when she first read *Black Feminist Thought*. Mary Romero, author of *Maid in the USA*, refers to "the publications of Judith Rollins, Evelyn Nakano Glenn, and Bonnie Thornton Dill" as shaping her work, particularly because of "how they interlocked race, gender, and class analysis."[56] And some scholars had an influence because they illustrated that members of communities formerly underrepresented in academia could achieve. Denise Segura, a pioneering scholar in Chicano studies, was stunned by the essays of Maxine Baca Zinn because, as she writes, "[I] thought to myself, 'My God, a Chicana has written an article and it's published. And a second one! Is that what I am supposed to do?' I started imagining writing about Chicanas and thinking that if one Chicana can do it then surely others could. Maybe. These were the first articles by a Chicana I had seen in journals. I had seen magazine articles, but I can't overstate the importance of this moment to a twenty-year-old undergraduate Chicana. It evoked the farmworker slogan by Dolores Huerta, 'Sí se puede' (It can be done)!"[57]

As these examples, chosen to represent change over time and shifts and turns in the field, illustrate, sociologists, like thinkers in other disciplines, also stand "on the shoulders of giants."

Mentors and Collaborators

Some observers believe that those who come from communities or positions underrepresented in academia need extra support to launch professional careers as they struggle to survive in what are often hostile environments. Andersen and Zinn, for example, write that sponsors— which they define as a "person who notices your talent . . . and introduces you to new possibilities for your life and career"—and mentors—persons who "provide intellectual and often personal support while giving information about career opportunities and possibly even financial assistance"—have been pivotal for the intellectual journeys and careers of the scholars who led the way in rethinking race and ethnicity.[58]

In addition to individual mentors and sponsors, collaboration has been especially important for scholars from marginalized communities. Bonnie Thornton Dill writes about a "scholarly sisterhood" that initially included Cheryl Townsend Gilkes and Elizabeth Higginbotham. Denise Segura mentions a group called La Collectiva, consisting of "Chicana graduate students, mostly from sociology, anthropology, history, and economics, as well as a few spouses of our male colleagues," that "did projects together." She continues that through collaboration they attained research skills on topics of interest to them even though they had no institutional support.[59] And Jennifer Pierce acknowledges the strong community consisting of feminist scholars at the University of Minnesota who bolstered her when she was first denied tenure.[60]

Career Paths

Whatever draws them in and supports their intellectual activity, not everyone has the same career in sociology. Older groups of sociologists, many of them founders in the field, almost all of them men, and most of them White, account for careers in essays that read like CVs prepared for a job application. They write about moments of success: I studied here, finished my dissertation to great acclaim there, got a job at this first-class university, and then, lo and behold, I moved to that job in an even more attractive setting. Take Seymour Martin Lipset as an example. After deciding that it was time for him to leave the University of California, Berkeley, he writes, because he had become "overly involved in Berkeley academic politics and administration as the Director of the Institute of International Studies and as a close adviser of the President of the University, Clark Kerr," he felt it was time for him to move to "Harvard University to become the George Markham Professor of Government and Sociology."[61]

Occasionally the men in these early generations of U.S. sociology complain about conflicts with others, about the absence of recognition, about having to move from one institution to another (sometimes after being denied tenure), and about feeling like an outsider within the field. But they rarely write about how class, race, and gender enabled or even shaped their aspirations, much less their scholarly interests and achievements. And, perhaps even less surprising (if often more annoying), they do not mention the multiple ways in which their careers depended on the labor of their wives and how they often intensified that labor by moving for purposes of career advancement or research opportunities.[62]

A few women in the first couple of generations also report having straightforward careers. But especially among an older group of predominantly White sociologists, women write about, in the apt phrase used by Darling in the introduction to *Journeys*, more "circuitous" careers shaped by discrimination and by not being taken (or not taking themselves) seriously. For some, the result is an academic life on the margins, in the less prestigious colleges and universities (which is not to say that those sites did not have their own considerable benefits). Many recount specific moments when sexism dislodged and uprooted their movement forward and, on some occasions, even being able to take credit for their own research. They write about the accommodations they had to make not just to keep a work-life "balance" but to manage any work at all. Some write about doing their "own" work in the early morning and late nights; they know that their lives fit uneasily into the framework of expectations set by institutions that did not recognize the demands of children, illness, dual careers, and caregiving. As noted already, older women speak eagerly and even joyfully about the discovery of feminist thought within sociology and of how it enabled them to understand the field better, to innovate in their own research, and to find a way to move forward.[63]

Notable examples stand out. Dorris W. Goodrich dropped out of academia because she could not combine work and responsibility for four children. Arlene Kaplan Daniels reports approaching Erving Goffman for help. His response, she writes, was "in fact, scathing." He said, "'You're not really a professional! You're only a homemaker looking for pin money.'" Not surprisingly, she remembers his "contempt vividly."[64] Only later, with the help of a feminist consciousness, did she come to recognize "the larger pattern in all the slights, snubs, omissions, and patronizing acts that [she] had shrugged off as [her] paranoia or [her] just desserts." Then, she tells us, "I felt rage at what I had endured and terrible sorrow for all that had hampered me."[65]

In the same collection of essays by Berkeley women sociologists that showcases pieces by Goodrich and Daniels, Dorothy E. Smith suggests that "it must be hard for women in academic life today to grasp just how the institutional order of patriarchy in the university was taken for granted—more than that, how deeply it was implicated in the established gender order beyond as well within the university." And she adds that men suffered too, as was the case for her husband for not achieving as well as his own wife, who succeeded in spite of the considerable odds against her.[66] In her classic essay "Inside the Clockwork of Male Careers," Arlie Russell Hochschild accounts for women's careers that had unexpected "twists and turns" because "the classic profile of the academic career is cut to the image of the traditional man with his traditional wife."[67] In short, early generations of White men in sociology did not notice the advantages that accrued to them. The women who were their contemporaries not only noted those advantages but acutely experienced disadvantages of exclusion and of being undervalued.

Both men and women from marginalized communities refer to the overt racism that denied them funds, positions, and opportunities. They write often (especially in Stanfield's *History of Race Relations Research: First Generation Recollections*) about the tension between being social activists and having academic careers.[68] Collections of essays by specific groups of scholars (Asian Americans, first-generation faculty of color, women of color in higher education, feminists, professors from working-class backgrounds) or by those from more diverse groupings (as represented in the two volumes of *Presumed Incompetent*) broaden the critique of sociology as a field and of academia as a site in which to launch and enjoy a career.[69] Contributors write of the contradiction between the notion that higher education is a "liberal" environment and the reality that it is an environment that is often, because of its uneven access to "privileges and hierarchies," a place of harassment and microaggressions. They speak of the uneven burden of advising and supporting students. They write about having to conform to expectations derived from class-based privileges or from the assumption that certain bodies (and certain expressions of gender) fit institutional norms better than others.[70] And they occasionally acknowledge that "those who have been victimized by various oppressions are still quite capable of oppressing others."[71]

With respect to sociology as a discipline, the scholars in these collections suggest both that major thinkers have been overlooked and that the inclusion of a wider range of voices can result in different questions being asked and different topics being studied. Occasionally they highlight the possibility and advantages of more varied ways of presenting their research (e.g., as poems or performances). And some go beyond those critiques to illustrate that transgender and nonbinary scholars can "disrupt the cisnormative assumptions of ethnographic fieldwork, of sociology, and of academia," thus generating "queer forms of knowledge production that center trans and non-binary experiences and perspectives and that move us toward thinking anew about researchers, embodiment, and methods, and their epistemological effects."[72]

Conclusion

Whether or not sociologists take full advantage of being both insiders and outsiders when they write memoirs, their writings provide insight into the many ways people have experienced the ideas of the field and their own individual place within it. Some tell stories of inspiration and individual effort resulting in graceful upward trajectories. Others acknowledge a less comfortable fit between who they are and what the field has to offer by way of concepts and career opportunities. Both individual characteristics (e.g., gender) and the historical moment of entry into the discipline (e.g., before or after feminist thought emerged) help explain many, if not all, of these differences. By reading these memoirs—whether in the form of a book or a shorter essay—students and professionals can better understand those who came before. They will then be equipped to make sense of (if not to write) their own sociological autobiographies, by placing their ideas, their individual challenges, and their careers in the appropriate historical context.

Curiously, although several of these many essays discuss at length the ideas motivating (and emerging from) research, few scholars focus on the conduct of research itself as a core activity of the life of a so-ciologist. Many dismiss, in a sentence or two, their first independent scholarly endeavor, which is usually their master's or doctorate the-sis. In the next chapter I turn to the ways in which three well-known scholars discuss an initial research project in book-length memoirs; these memoirs describe both the research process itself and, in two cases, a scholar's response to the reception of that research as evalu-ative criteria changed. They thus offer insights into how to confront issues of methods and assessment.

4

The Research

Among the memoirists discussed in the previous chapter, W. E. B. Du Bois, William F. Whyte, and Renée Fox stand out because they used their autobiographical writing as an occasion to reflect deeply on their own scholarship and, more specifically, on an early piece of independent research. I ask a series of questions about these memoirs. What insights do these three scholars offer that can help us understand the experience of learning how to do sociology? What issues do they raise in retrospect that can help us better evaluate our methods? How do they make sense of the reception of their work? Do they respond to changes in the field? And what do they omit that we might want them to pursue?

I turn first to W. E. B. Du Bois, who published three separate autobiographies: *Darkwater: Voices from Within the Veil* (1920), *Dusk of Dawn* (1940), and *The Autobiography of W. E. B. Du Bois: A Soliloquy on Viewing My Life from the Last Decade of Its First Century* (1962), written when he was in his nineties.[1] In all three he comments on *The Philadelphia Negro* (*TPN*), one of his first pieces of independent scholarship, published in 1889, over thirty years before he wrote his first autobiography.[2] William H. Whyte conducted the research that resulted in *Street Corner Society* (*SCS*) as a "junior fellow" at Harvard University, immediately after his graduation from Swarthmore College; the book first appeared in 1943.[3] Almost half a century later, in 1994, his autobiography, *Participant Observer*, was published. In her 2011 autobiography, *In the Field: A Sociologist's Journey*, Renée Fox describes the research she conducted over fifty years earlier when she was a graduate student in social relations at Harvard University studying under the mentorship of Talcott

Parsons.[4] Subsequently she published that work as *Experiment Perilous*
(*EP*) in 1959.[5]

All three of these sociologists studied at Harvard University. All three
of their original works (*TPN*, *SCS*, *EP*) were of groundbreaking significance and received positive reviews when they were first published, although all three also had moments of being ignored by scholars working
in similar areas of investigation. And given the gap between their early
scholarship and their autobiographies, all three authors had the opportunity to reflect on their work and reconsider its virtues—and its flaws.

W. E. B. Du Bois, *The Philadelphia Negro*

Du Bois opens his first two pieces of autobiographical writing by linking
his life story to the story of all African Americans in the United States.
He opens his third with the description of his fifteenth trip abroad. In
all three, Du Bois discusses the research experience that led to *TPN*; in
these discussions he includes comments both on his personal evaluation
of it and on its critical reception.

In 1896, after fourteen years of teaching at Wilberforce University,
the University of Pennsylvania offered Du Bois a position to be held
for one year without either an office or any "official recognition of any
kind."[6] Despite these constraints, Du Bois jumped at the opportunity to
work in sociology and, more specifically, to study Philadelphia's "Negro
Seventh Ward." Having accepted the position, he moved his new bride
to a one-room apartment over a cafeteria in what was considered "the
worst part of the Seventh Ward." There they lived for a year, in what
Du Bois described as "an atmosphere of dirt, drunkenness, poverty, and
crime."[7]

Du Bois was far from naïve when he set out to do the work that led
to *TPN*. He recognized "that the city of Philadelphia at that time had a
theory; and that theory was that this great, rich, and famous municipal-
ity was going to the dogs because of the crime and venality of its Negro
citizens, who lived largely centered in the slum at the lower end of the

seventh ward." And he knew that he had been appointed to "prove this by figures." But he did not care. He had his own goal: "I saw only here a chance to study an historical group of black folk and to show exactly what their place was in the community."[8]

Despite what he understood to be some significant barriers, he was eager to enter the field. Without any advice about either "research methods" or "procedure," he began his study, committed to doing all the work on his own: "I studied it personally and not by proxy. I sent out no canvassers. I went myself. Personally I visited and talked with 5,000 persons. . . . I went through the Philadelphia libraries for data, gained access in many instances to private libraries of colored folk and got individual information. I mapped the district classifying it by conditions; I compiled two centuries of the history of the Negro in Philadelphia and in the Seventh Ward."[9]

He soon ran into trouble. He is refreshingly frank about the initial confusion that swept over him as he collected massive amounts of data: "The world seized and whirled me. I hardly knew what was important, what negligible." He is equally frank about his initial reception and how the hostility of the residents added to his confusion: "The colored people of Philadelphia received me with no open arms. They had a natural dislike to being studied like a strange species. I met again and in different guise those curious cross-currents and inner social whirlings. They set me to groping. I concluded that I did not know so much as I might about my own people . . . [and was] painfully aware that merely being born in a group, does not necessarily make one possessed of complete knowledge concerning it."[10]

But neither his initial confusion nor this hostile reception deterred him. In a mere dozen months, he completed his study, understanding now that his life work was to further understand what the study had revealed: "the Negro group as a symptom, not a cause; as a striving, palpitating group, and not an inert sick body of crime; as a long historic development and not a transient occurrence." Not yet the critic of capitalism that he would become later in his life, Du Bois demonstrates how the history of slavery and ongoing prejudice with their links to relationships within the Black community could explain why African Americans had not yet made the advances they would have hoped. And in so doing he challenges the eugenic theories of the day, locating the problems of African Americans not in their "heredity" but in the social conditions confronting them.

Putting aside what he knew to be the insult of not being offered an instructorship at the University of Pennsylvania, Du Bois in 1899 put before the American Academy a plan for further study, even as he acknowledged the limitations of sociological research as he had experienced them while writing *TPN*. That is, in this plan he included a critique of his own methods. He aims the first part of this critique at statistics: "The best available methods of sociological research are at present so liable to inaccuracies that the careful student discloses the results of individual research with diffidence; he knows that they are liable to error from the seemingly ineradicable faults of the statistical method." He then moves on to what he considers the "greater error from the methods of general observation." "Above all," he continues, the researcher "must ever tremble lest some personal bias, some moral conviction or some unconscious trend of thought due to previous training, has to a degree distorted the picture in his view." He understands that freedom from bias is impossible: "Convictions on all great matters of human interest one must have to a greater or less degree, and they will enter to some extent into the most cold-blooded scientific research as a disturbing factor." Even so, having acknowledged inevitable weaknesses, he still expresses his conviction that his kind of research must be done: "We must study, we must investigate, we must attempt to solve; and the utmost that the world can demand is, not lack of human interest and moral conviction, but rather the heart-quality of fairness and an earnest desire for the truth despite its possible unpleasantness."[11]

Taken together, these reflections highlight issues relevant to the conduct of sociological research. Du Bois acknowledges the change in perception and understanding that emerges through deep engagement in the field. He openly accepts the limitations of his statistical methods and even more openly acknowledges (although he does not enumerate them) the limitations stemming from individual biases. He recognizes the objectification of studying people "like animals" and comes to understand that being part of a social group does not necessarily translate into an understanding of that group. Finally, he looks back on how his work was received and evaluated. He is "consoled" by the fact that even if, as he believes, "few persons ever read that fat volume," TPN itself is treated "with respect."[12]

Although Du Bois is frank about the limitations emerging from inadequate statistical methods and personal biases, he only hints at the issues of how his social class might have shaped his reception by the community he chose to study. Subsequent scholars have noted that he must have cut a strange figure in Philadelphia's Seventh Ward. For example, professor of American studies Maria Diedrich describes him as "an almost extremely proper and rather stiff young scholar, always dressed in a suit and starched shirt and usually wearing gloves" as he "delved deeply into this heavily congested and noisy black community." No surprise, she writes, that "most of the interviewed responded only reluctantly to his questions; it seems that they were unable to accept this unusually well dressed and well educated black gentleman as 'one of us,' and in several instances doors were violently slammed into his face."[13]

Du Bois also remains oblivious to issues of gender. He does not say whether men or women responded differently to him; he does not apologize for having brought his young wife to live in difficult surroundings; and he omits entirely any mention of a study on domestic service written by Isabel Eaton and appended to TPN. A century later, Diedrich asks about this last omission: "What was the relationship between Eaton and Du Bois? How did he feel about University of Pennsylvania Press publishing her research in one volume with his, and how did she respond when her text was reduced to a mere adjunct? Was the working relationship continued after 1897?"[14] For all the honesty and forthrightness of Du Bois's writings, these questions have no answers.

William Foote Whyte, *Street Corner Society*

Whyte opens his memoir with the observation that the titles for his books always came last, after a long struggle. But not, he says, in the case of this piece of autobiographical writing: "'Participant Observer' not only conveys the research style for which I am best known, but in a sense, it also describes who I am and have been. . . . This is a book on what I have learned from observing myself."[15] So, we might ask, what in fact had he learned as he reflected on the research that resulted in the book known as *Street Corner Society*? And what can he teach us?

The facts are these. Immediately after finishing college, Whyte joined the ranks of the junior fellows at Harvard with a three-year grant to do whatever he wanted. From the start he knew he wanted to "study a slum district." He made the choice of Boston's North End, as he puts it, on "very unscientific grounds." It *looked* like a slum to him. And so, like Du Bois, he sallied forth. After several false starts Ernest Pecci ("Doc" in his book) agreed to provide Whyte with entrée into the community. Soon Whyte became aware that rather than commuting between the North End and Cambridge, he needed to immerse himself in the community, so he began lodging with a family, which alleviated some of the strain of doing field work.[16] When he married, as did Du Bois, he moved his bride into an apartment in the research site.

Also like Du Bois, Whyte writes openly, not only of issues of acceptance in the community (and of occasional errors made) but also of the confusion of the first stages of conducting research. He confesses that it took eighteen months "before I knew what I was doing." During that time, he also confesses, he worried about his decision to do little "formal interviewing": "Sometimes I wondered whether just hanging out on the street corner was an active enough process to be dignified by the term 'research.' I wondered whether I should be asking questions." But initially he did not really know "when to question and when not to, . . . as well as what questions to ask." Gradually, however, he began to "adjust the sensitiveness of the questions to the strength of my relationship with

THE RESEARCH | 71

the informant." During these early months he took pleasure in every sign that the young men he studied regarded him as a "fixture" and was thrilled when they allowed him to take his turn in an important baseball game. Even so, from time to time, he fretted that his efforts to fit in had been too successful: he feared he had moved from "nonparticipating observer" to "nonobserving participant."[17]

Whyte was dismayed when, after two years of research, he found that he would have only a one-year extension to his fellowship. In retrospect, however, he decided this was a good thing, bringing him to conclude that a "community study has no logical end point." He quickly completed the first draft of his manuscript, showed it to Pecci (whose criticisms, he said, "were invaluable"), and soon thereafter left for Chicago to study with W. Lloyd Warner.

Whyte tells the story of the research for *SCS* both in the appendix to its 1955 edition and in several chapters of his 1994 memoir. In the penultimate chapter of the latter, Whyte returns to a discussion of *SCS*, noting that although the "early reactions of my sociological colleagues [had been] disappointing," the appendix gave the book "a new lease on life" and that the subsequent paperback edition "boosted sales to a new high."[18]

If the book had not initially had a profound effect on the field, he wrote, it had had a "profound effect" on him. It had helped him bring his values in line with his scholarship. He also came to "like and respect [himself] more" through the relationships he formed while doing research. And he had learned to be patient during what he called the "long dormant period" when he didn't know what to write: "I came to expect that when I did not understand what I was observing, the underlying pattern would reveal itself if I just kept active in the field and kept on writing."[19]

But Whyte had more to say about *SCS* when the book became the subject of two sets of critiques in the 1990s.[20] The first set appeared in a book called *Reframing Organizational Culture* (*ROC*), in which essays by four behavioral scientists "hailed the book as a classic" but also raised some methodological issues Whyte found "worth discussing."[21] The second, in the *Journal of Contemporary Ethnography* (*JCE*), included half a dozen essays and an introduction by Patricia Adler, Peter Adler, and John M. Johnson.[22]

The critiques in *ROC* and in *JCE* take several different forms. In *JCE* W. A. Marianne Boelen challenges *SCS* from start to finish. She accuses Whyte of incorrect interpretations, of factual misrepresentation, and of unethical relationships with his informants.[23] In particular, with respect to the latter, she writes that he abused his relationship with Pecci and that he did not sufficiently credit Pecci's contribution. In his direct response to her, Whyte itemizes what he claims are *Boelen's* errors on all her points. He also "corrects" what he calls "miscellaneous errors and misinterpretations." In short, he defends *SCS* on the grounds of "truth."[24]

Other commentators take quite a different approach. Norm Denzin critiques Whyte *and* Boelen. Denzin explains that because neither Whyte nor Boelen is willing to "take up the challenge" of "poststructuralism" but both still "want a world out there that proves their theory right or wrong," he rejects each of them.[25] Writing in *ROC*, Riley argues along the same lines, questioning whether there is any "culture organization 'out there' to be accurately represented by observers."[26] Laurel Richardson similarly castigates Whyte and Boelen in *JCE* from a "postfoundational sensibility," which requires the author to locate the "construction of knowledge in humanly situated social practices." She would have preferred, she writes, to have seen Whyte do more to account for how his social position shaped the information he obtained and the analysis he provided. It was insufficient that he noted his class position, educational status, and liberal bent. He should also have acknowledged that his race and gender mattered: "being White and Male," she insists, "were the necessary tickets for entry."[27]

Whyte cedes some ground to these critics: "Reflecting on 'postfoundational' ethnology, I have come to recognize that the objective-subjective distinction is not as clear as I once thought. Though my study of the social structure of street corner gangs was based primarily upon direct observation, researchers cannot observe everything, and if we tried, we would end up with miscellaneous data, which would yield no intelligible pattern. We seek to observe behavior that is significant to our research purposes. Selection therefore depends upon some implicit or explicit theory—a process that is in large part subjective." But he is not willing to concede altogether. The choice of what to observe, he says, is "not random." He continues, "If we specify our theoretical assumptions and the research methods we use, others can utilize the same assumptions and methods to either verify or challenge our conclusions." And while he believes that the standards of critical epistemology "may have served a useful purpose in the postcolonial era by inviting outside observers to question their own assumptions of a given culture and to seek the views of members of that culture," he rejects those standards, believing that an outsider "can make important contributions." More significantly, he believes that scientific arguments are not "just" literary criticism. That approach, he argues, is a "dead end" and "a passing fad." In time, he concludes, "behavioral scientists who have succumbed to that lure will return to the pursuit of scientific knowledge."[28]

Whyte thus had a rich opportunity to engage with his critics. In his response, he models a capacity to learn from and to respond openly to them even if he goes only so far and then fundamentally disagrees. Explicitly (as Du Bois did implicitly), he rejects the necessity for a throughgoing consideration of how his personal attributes (White, upper-middle-class, highly-educated, male) shaped his reception in the community and the content of what he did (and did not) learn. And he rejects the standards of what he calls "critical epistemology" as he defends (much as Du Bois might have done for *TPN* even as he acknowledged its limitations) the "scientific basis" of the scholarship on which *SCS* rested.

Renée Fox, *Experiment Perilous*

In the introduction to her memoir Renée Fox writes that the work "on which I am embarking is a love story in several respects—love of my life as a sociologist, in the classrooms, hospital wards, clinics, and medical laboratories. . . . It is also a love story about my relationship to those who have accompanied me along the mysterious, unlikely but chosen and committed path I have traveled."[29] Having offered one account of her writing, she soon offers another: drawing back from the notion that this is either an autobiography or memoir "in the usual senses of those terms," she suggests that "it might be more accurate to call it an *ethnography*—an *ethnography of the life of a sociologist*."[30] This approach, she adds, makes her feel that it is "less like a self-absorbed, ego-driven endeavor" and that by "making [her] life as a sociologist the object of study and narration, [she is] joining hands . . . with all the persons who have been participating subjects of [her] research, and who people the pages [she has] written." She thus gives us permission to read her memoir as we would an ethnography, asking about the depth of her observations as well as her blind spots and raising questions about what she did, and did not, include in her retrospective gaze.

Fox's research story goes like this. Initially through the intermediary of Talcott Parsons, Dr. Henry M. Fox (no relation), the psychiatrist-in-chief at the Peter Bent Brigham Hospital in Boston, offered Fox the job of studying "the relationship between the patient-subjects [on a ward of critically ill patients], and the milieux of their families." Huffy because she wanted to distance herself from the idea that women, even (or perhaps especially) when they were sociologists, should be interested in families, she began to turn him down. Yet as they talked, she learned about a kind of community among the "residents" of the ward (an Adrenalectomy Club among the men who had had their adrenal glands removed) that she recognized as being like the Half-Lung Club from her reading of Thomas Mann's *Magic Mountain*. In a quick reversal she accepted the job and initiated her months of ethnography observing both the patients on the ward and the physicians treating those patients.

In her memoir, she describes in detail the moment she came to believe the patients on the ward accepted her. When she was asked a question about whether she was "a polio" (by one of the men who had noticed her uncertain gait), she tells us that she "assumed that in a setting like [the ward], when such a question was asked, you were expected to answer it with matter-of-fact candor."[31] She concludes that her honesty—and her shared experience with a medical issue—smoothed the way to acceptance and to openness about "the harsh realities of being a patient." At the same time, if having been a patient might have eased her entry into confidences, she recognizes that being a woman might have created more complications. Yet she insists that was not the case even though the patients who saw her as a "'nice girl' and a 'lady'" excluded her from "what they called their 'torrid sessions' of 'male talk and joking,' primarily 'about sex.'" Fox is less explicit about how she gained entry to the community of (all male) physicians as they gathered daily for evening rounds or how she acquired permission to read the notes in patient charts. She simply implies that there too she had uncensored access to the feelings of the participants.

Fox openly shares the ways in which spending time with patients who were critically ill took its toll: "There were interludes while I was on the ward conducting my field research when I had profound difficulty coping with my feelings about the predicament of the patients. I lost a lot of weight. And at one point I developed what physicians of that era would probably have diagnosed as 'angioneurotic edema' . . . caused by stress, and possibly my over-identification with the edematous state of many of the patients." In fact, so distraught was she when one of the patients died that she was not only unable to record her observations but also "shaken by doubts about the justification and usefulness of [her] research and, beyond that, about the ultimate meaning of being a sociologist."[32] Although she insists she "surmounted this crisis," she chose not to revisit the ward while she was attempting to write about it.

In an enviably brief period, Fox completed her dissertation to the enthusiastic response of her advisor. However, the physician who had allowed her access to the ward also read that work. When she spoke with him, he "questioned the validity of [her] descriptive analysis of the patient community" and was "even more critical of the veracity of [her] sociological portrait of the team of research physicians." He argued that the dissertation was too critical of the ward and should not be approved without major revisions and then, even if rewritten, should be "listed as a document that had limited circulation, and was available only by special request."[33]

Fox's autobiography reveals this and other critical moments in her research process essentially in the order in which they occurred: these include the "aha" of recognizing that there's something there to study; the anxiety of entering the field; the consequential decision to offer or withhold information about oneself; the delight of believing that the participants are open in your presence (whether true or not); the emotional stress of observing people in difficult situations; the satisfaction of receiving approval by those in a position to judge; and the dismay of a negative reaction. And by recounting them, she provides opportunities for identification and an opening for discussion.

Fox interrogates other significant aspects of her research in a revised (1997) edition of *EP* that includes a "new epilogue." One set of reflections concerns the contrast between what she thinks of as objectivity and science on the one hand and what she thinks of as compassion on the other. She notes how unusual her research was at the time in which she conducted it: "Not only was there no precedent for such an inquiry, but its legitimacy was questionable. Neither the moral justification for this type of study nor its social scientific meaningfulness was established. If anything, the academic medical and social scientific climate of the 1950s ran counter to it."[34]

Twenty years later, Fox finds the climate has changed, offering a more welcoming home for her approach: "Although the canon of scientific objectivity still guides medical and social research," she writes, "criticism of the 'dehumanization' that an overly detached approach can effect is more frequently heard. There is less of a tendency to view 'involvement' exclusively as a methodological aberration." She continues, in its efforts to "infuse objectivity with compassion," "[*Experiment Perilous*] is more contemporaneous now than it was at the time of its initial publication."[35]

Fox describes a second element of a changing climate. The 1950s, she reminds us, "was a time of great enthusiasm about clinical medical research." Although "memories of the Nazi medical war crimes were still hauntingly present . . . the renaissance of medical research was incompatible with sustained brooding about the ethicality of human experimentation under various conditions, or about the social and cultural questions that it raised." Two decades later, she writes, medicine had become more concerned with the "ethical and existential issues related to biomedical advance, the delivery of medical care, and medical decision-making in general is now more salient in medicine in social science." In a 1995 address (included in the 2011 edition of *EP*) Fox reiterates this shift, noting that at the time of her research no institutional review boards (IRBs) existed to evaluate (and curb) the experimentation conducted at the hospital and on the metabolic ward. Although Fox remains protective of the physicians with whom she worked during her research, we might ask whether an IRB would allow *any* experimentation without informed consent. We might also ask about the ethics of *her* research on the ward where she came to know the patients and physicians intimately. But it seems, even in 2011 when IRBs were evaluating just this kind of research, Fox raises no concerns about what she had done and how she had done it.

Finally, we might raise some significant methodological issues about gender. Can we as easily as she did dismiss the impact of gender on how the patients regarded her? How did gender enter her relationships with male physicians? And was gender relevant to her having excluded the nursing staff from the study? In short, we might ask what a more gendered perspective would have added.

According to historian Emily K. Abel, "By the late 1950s, a growing number of academics and health professionals began to criticize . . . the lack of attention to the needs of patients approaching finality." Abel cites "landmark works" that "helped to shape" the field of "patients' perspectives."[36] Curiously, when scholars began to advocate for others to include the patients' point of view, none referenced the earlier work by Fox, which had done just that. For her part, Fox says little about whether she thought sociologists in the field "slighted" her work.

Summing Up

Du Bois, Whyte, and Fox are all self-protective, proud of moments of hard work and insight, and disappointed by moments of being overlooked or critiqued. None of the three is particularly attentive to their own positioning, to how their race, class, gender, sexuality, or ability shaped access to research sites, their observations, and their analysis. None, in more than glancing ways, examines defects and limitations. In fact, when those are noted, Whyte, from whom we have the most extensive writing about these issues, responds with vigor, defending his choices and the completed research.

Along with occasional defensiveness, each of the three allowed rare access into the constraints, impediments, and indecisions—along with the joys and satisfactions—of conducting and publishing sociological research. Du Bois and Whyte both confronted time limits. Du Bois was hired for just a year; Whyte ran out of resources when he still wanted to remain in the field. Without a logical end point, Whyte reminds us, sometimes we finish research not because it is "done" but because we must be done.

Du Bois and Whyte both tell us that they did not know what they were doing for much of the time they were doing it, sharing the frustration—and necessity—of being open to the confusions of the first stages of a research project; they also tell us that from time to time they had doubts about what they were doing and whether it really constituted research. Both also openly acknowledge mistakes in the ways they approached informants, while Fox openly shares the emotional costs of involvement with her research "subjects." Whyte and Fox both, albeit in separate ways, resist more contemporary readings or evaluations of their scholarship.

In the introduction to *Open to Disruption*, a collection of essays on conducting a single research project over an extended period, Margaret K. Nelson and Rosanna Hertz write,

> For all the discussion about the research process in social science, few accounts open up that process to inspection. Rather, most published descriptions of the research process take a standard narrative form: an idea for study, followed by data collection, analysis, and writing. This narrative assumes a smooth, continuous arc that invariably ends with publication (otherwise we wouldn't be reading it). Someone has finished a project, sent it off into the world, and is now ready to move on to the next item on the academic agenda. The trajectory of the arc appears set from the beginning. The dynamic way in which our craft actually evolves is rarely chronicled and the backstage stories remain hallway talk at professional meetings or uncomfortable silences we keep to ourselves.[37]

In *their* memoirs, Du Bois, Whyte, and Fox did something different: they made their own research process available to retrospective evaluation, exploring both defects and moments of confusion as well as holding on to, and lauding, their significant achievements. These are rare gifts, and gifts that are likely to make us all better at our craft.

PART III

Sociological Uses of Memoirs

5

Memoirs as Education

In *The Wounded Storyteller*, sociologist Arthur Frank makes a distinction between thinking "with" a story and thinking "about" it.[1] When we think *with* a story, Frank argues, we take the story as it is and do not seek to go beyond it. We allow it to affect us and to identify those aspects of our lives we share with the storyteller. Our response is more emotional than intellectual. By way of contrast, thinking *about* a story involves analyzing the content for the broader themes, concepts, and issues it presents. Here we let our intellect get the better of our emotions. In what follows, I suggest that this tidy distinction, useful as it may be for some purposes, will—and even should—break down when we read memoirs to gain insights into sociology.[2] To be effective in creating empathy and exciting the imagination, memoirs must move their readers to identify with and be open to the ideas of the memoir writer. At the same time, if we are to learn sociology from memoirs, we must stand back and ask about the categories, subjects, or patterns the memoir illustrates. At this point, the sociological imagination might come into play, as we place the individual story in its appropriate social context and draw on relevant concepts to make analytic links.

To illustrate this merging of reading *with* and thinking *about*, I focus here on why and how we might read memoirs to gain insight into central ideas and issues in sociology. I discuss how sociologists at every stage can draw on memoirs to make sense of key concepts as they are exposed to experiences that may be similar to or, perhaps even more often, quite different from their own. First, I examine several memoirs about childhoods in which the authors consciously embed a sociological lens.

I then turn to memoirs written by those who do not make explicit the sociological significance of their experiences. I point out some specific challenges involved in learning from each of these.[3] I then discuss more generally the reasons for and against relying on memoirs for the acquisition and development of a sociological imagination. Finally, I suggest questions to guide our reading and discussions of memoirs.[4]

Some Examples

Memoirs written by sociologists can be an especially helpful learning tool when the authors carefully apply a sociological framework to highlight central issues.[5] Several illustrative examples come to mind. Dalton Conley's autobiographical *Honky* is perhaps the best-known memoir written by a sociologist.[6] Conley, who is White, tells the story of his childhood living in an almost exclusively Black community (what he calls "the Projects"). In this memoir, Conley self-consciously explains how he came to understand the enormous social significance of race. When he describes his experiences attending predominantly White schools, he similarly, self-consciously, identifies how he came to better understand the meaning and importance of social class.[7] Perhaps because the "sociology" is so prominent here, this book has frequently been used in the classroom.[8] One professor, Brian Kapitulik, offers undergraduate students an assignment that helps underline the book's sociological significance: "Choose FOUR 'particular experiences' from Conley's life and explain how each experience relates to the 'invisible contours of inequality.' You are free to choose whichever experiences you wish but I'd like you to use the following themes (which were mainstays of this course) as a guide: 1) White Privilege; 2) Cultural Capital; 3) Education; 4) Social Class Mobility; 5) The 'America Dream'; 6) Institutionalized Racism; 7) The Intersections of Race and Class." As the wording of this assignment indicates, Kapitulik finds *Honky* a convenient way to help us "discern the relationships between social factors and personal experience in *someone else's life*." By reading *Honky*, Kapitulik suggests, we can learn to place another's experience in a broader social context before we try to do the same with our own.[9]

Other sociologists have also written memoirs that openly offer sociological reflections. We could learn from them as well. Michael A. Messner's *King of the Wild Suburb: A Memoir of Fathers, Sons and Guns* explores the difficulty boys might have in adopting a form of masculinity different from that of their fathers.[10] Mindy Fried's memoir about caring for her aging father, *Caring for Red*, raises the challenges of caregiving as well as the challenges of aging in our world today.[11] Deborah Cohan's *Welcome to Wherever We Are: A Memoir of Family, Caregiving, and Redemption* touches on some of the same issues and asks the hard question about what we owe to those who have abused us.[12] Grace Cho's memoir, *Tastes Like War*, makes repeated reference to significant sociological issues like stigma, culture, racism, and consumption.[13] In *A Boy's Journey: From Nazi-Occupied Prague to Freedom in America* (and in an accompanying essay), Peter Stein is explicit about how his experiences helped him develop a "sociological eye."[14] Finally, although originally written as a blog, Erik Olin Wright's *Stardust to Stardust* occasionally analyzes the ways in which the organization of the hospital in which he received treatment for his intractable leukemia allowed personal relationships to develop that enhanced the provision of care.[15]

While we might expect that sociologists would be especially attuned to the links between individual experiences and social contexts, several recent memoirs written by other people include much of the same kind of analysis; they too can help us make sense of broader conceptional issues. For example, John Hendrickson's *Life on Delay* includes interviews with others who, like himself, have stuttered, and he identifies the experience as one of stigma, thereby transcending his own personal encounters.[16] Alice Robb's memoir, *Don't Think, Dear: On Loving and Leaving Ballet*, simultaneously narrates her own experiences and reveals the culture of the world of ballet, with its constraints on women, its creation of eating disorders, and its intense misogyny.[17] Books like these draw us in, highlight complex concepts, and place individual experiences within a broader framework. In short, these authors do some of the difficult analytical work that helps engender the sociological imagination.

However, since few sociologists have written this type of memoir, it might be difficult to find appropriate examples for the full range of issues we study in sociology. But there are many memoirs that, without explicitly embedding any kind of analytic lens, might also help us gain sociological insights. When I was teaching a "Sociology of the Family" course, I frequently used the memoir *Sleeping Arrangements* by Laura Shaine Cunningham.[18] My predominantly White and predominately very privileged students drew on their own experiences to understand the family; hence many tended to believe that most families resembled what Dorothy Smith has called the standard North American family, a family headed by a heterosexual couple and with a wage-earning father and a stay-at-home mother.[19] They thus assumed that only people quite different from themselves—people of color, people who were poor—experienced other family configurations. Cunningham's book introduced them to a White (Jewish) girl who initially lived alone with her mother who worked full-time outside the home and then, after her mother died, lived with two very peculiar uncles. Her great autonomy— running around on her own during the day, observing adult sex, jumping from building to building—challenged my students' prevailing notions of what constituted a family and of the "best" way to raise a child. At other times I used Mary Childers's *Welfare Brat* both to illuminate a life in poverty and to contest the notion that only African Americans rely on welfare.[20]

More recently, a broad array of memoirs reveals the ways in which an individual's background characteristics shape their life. On the issue of race and ethnicity alone, these include (among a vast number of others) Toni Jensen's *Carry: A Memoir of Survival on Stolen Land*, about being Native American; Joseph Earl Thomas's *Sink: A Memoir*, about growing up poor and Black in a Philadelphia neighborhood; and Alvin Eng's *Our Laundry, Our Town: My Chinese American Life from Flushing to the Downtown Stage and Beyond*, about life in a Chinese American family.[21]

Other memoirs introduce struggles with addiction, lives shaped by illness and disability, experiences of abuse, and time spent as an incarcerated person. The range of topics is almost endless; the specific issues at stake will determine the most appropriate examples.

These memoirs require that we do the work of analysis ourselves by asking questions about the links between individual experiences and social structures. Again, we can be guided by how others have approached this kind of work. For example, Jamie Oslawski-Lopez asked her undergraduate students to read *I Am Malala: How One Girl Stood Up for Education and Changed the World.*[22] In her discussion of the writing assignment that accompanied this reading, Oslawski-Lopez offers helpful prompts. She asked students to consider whether Malala was a "deviant," to think about how an understanding of the My Lai massacre could help engender an understanding of the Taliban gunman, and to discuss the different "tools" with which Malala formed her sense of self.

Brent Harger and Tim Hallett explain why they considered *The Autobiography of Malcolm X* an ideal way to begin to learn sociology.[23] That book, they write, is "partly a story about individual transformation and change" and partly "a story about the social structures that enabled and constrained this individual journey." Usefully, they also offer a specific example of *how* to draw on this book to better understand how the social structure affects individuals. They take an excerpt in which Malcolm X interacts with a teacher who discourages his dreams of becoming a lawyer and suggests instead he think about working with his hands. Following that interaction, Malcolm X realizes that the teacher had encouraged White children to aim for professional careers and that although he knew he was smarter than most of them, he would need to rely on his own ambition and not the help of others if he were to achieve his goals. After reading this excerpt, Harger and Hallett ask students to discuss three questions about this incident: "(1) Where in the excerpt can we see individual actions and decisions? (This is the class definition for 'human agency.') (2) Where in the excerpt can we see the weight of society, things that are beyond one's immediate control but that exert a force on one's life? (This is the definition for 'social structure' in the class.) (3) How can we understand the relationship between the two? (Thinking with the sociological imagination.)" The teachers then suggest that we can find direct links between the excerpt and four additional sociological concepts: "prejudice, discrimination, racism, and institutional racism."[24]

In short, in comparison with learning from memoirs written by sociologists, memoirs that are not explicitly sociological require more work before we are able to discern whether, and how, a particular piece of writing is relevant to a sociological theme.[25] But this seeming disadvantage can also be an advantage as we engage in creative interpretation and make discoveries on our own. Also, as noted, because existing memoirs cover such a wide variety of topics they can help us better understand a wide variety of issues.[26]

How Can Memoirs Enhance Our Sociological Thinking?

Let us consider more specifically how memoirs can help us learn sociology. Most importantly and most generally, as has been implied already, memoirs can help with the development of a sociological imagination as we begin to understand how to relate individual life experiences to structural forces.[27] In fact, scholars Katherine Mack and Jonathan Alexander believe that this linkage is intrinsic to memoir itself: "What is at stake in memoir," they write, "is the memoirist's (re)presentation of an individual and often exemplary life *in relation to larger political structures*."[28] And they provide evidence of this "stake" in their careful comparison of the implicit arguments embedded in two well-known and controversial memoirs—J. D. Vance's *Hillbilly Elegy* and Ta-Nehisi Coates's *Between the World and Me*.[29] In short, when we consider the forces shaping an individual's experiences, we might begin to question individual agency and its relationship to social constraints (including social norms) as well as social opportunities.

Memoirs can help us learn sociology in other ways. They can provide knowledge of worlds beyond our own firsthand experience, thereby enabling insight into different social environments and diverse cultures. For example, memoirs about growing up in the South, like bell hooks's *Bone Black: Memories of Girlhood* and Henry Louis Gates Jr.'s *Colored People*, bring to life the experience of segregation.[30] Memoirs can also provide a historical perspective, enabling us to explore how events in the past bear a striking (and surprising) similarity to events in the present. As an example, Peter Stein's *A Boy's Journey* can provide a jumping-off point for connecting "stories of the Holocaust with the hate crimes of today."[31]

Stein's memoir explores what it was like to be a Jewish boy in Germany before World War II; it thus focuses on a relatively narrow set of identities. But some memoirs explore even more complex intersections of selves: Christian Cooper, in *Better Living through Birding: Notes from a Black Man in the Natural World*, identifies himself as a birder, nerd, and bicyclist as well as a gay Black man living in New York City.[32] Through examining memoirs written by individuals who navigate multiple social locations, we can gain a deeper understanding of how these intersecting identities influence social experiences and shape social inequalities.

Memoirs can also expose us to a broader range of emotions and types of relationships than we might otherwise have personal experience with.[33] And by reading a series of memoirs on a single topic we can better view a condition—like mental illness—from the perspectives of a variety of different social positions: social workers, patients, doctors, family members, and people who do not seek treatment (or who do not even think of their illness as a "condition").[34]

Like fiction, memoirs can touch and move readers if we allow them to affect us in these ways. That is, if we engage in imaginative identification with an "other," memoirs can help with the development of empathy.[35] The abstract issues of significance to sociologists thus acquire a human face.[36] And as we make sense of, and identify with, the lives of others, we might also make a different kind of sense and evaluation of our own lives. Memoirs can thus create self-understanding.[37]

Memoirs can also provide the basis for interesting discussions about the complexities of the concept of "truth." Harger and Hallett, for example, note that the fictional aspect of autobiography impinges on how we interpret particular events. When they teach about Malcolm X, they raise the question of whether he really had the reported conversation with a teacher, whether, if so, those words were the precise ones used, and how and even whether the "truth" mattered.[38]

At a more practical (less theoretical) level, studies have shown that memoirs can engage readers in important ways that extend beyond adding variety.[39] Even if the orientation is different from our own, works that do not appear to be actively promoting a specific political agenda are less likely to make us defensive. At the same time, we need to learn how to read critically enough to understand those orientations. However, because memoirs are easier to read than strictly academic texts, we can more easily share ideas about important concepts.[40] In fact, studies have demonstrated that students who read nontraditional texts in a classroom outperform those who do not.[41]

As with other literature, reading memoirs can cause discomfort and anxiety. Whether or not trigger warnings are in place, and whether or not trigger warnings protect an audience, memoirs might use language and raise issues that some find difficult.[42] But discomfort can also enhance learning if we probe the reasons for our feelings.

Interrogating Memoir

Of course no one reads Conlon's *Honky*—or any other memoir—and instantaneously develops a sociological imagination.[43] In addition to the questions mentioned above with respect to specific works, a series of questions that guide the reading of memoirs can aid in the development of the skill of critical reading *from a sociological perspective*.[44]

Recall that in a previous chapter I examined ways of thinking about the self who tells a story. To guide the reading of memoirs, we might ask specifically about the relationships among the various "selves" identified by Smith and Watson, as illustrated in the questions in box 5.1.[45]

Box 5.1: Selves

Who is the author? What do we know about that "flesh and blood" person? Where did they live? How do we assess the extent to which an author is "accurate" about the details of their past?

What choices did the narrating "I" make? How did those choices shape (or limit) what the memoir includes?

Does the narrating "I" acknowledge limits to memory? What events and emotions do you think might be unavailable to the narrator because of those limits?[46]

What kind of self does the memoir portray here? Which part of the "self" did the author choose to narrate and why? Which part of the self did the author omit and why?

What framework motivates and then constrains the presentation of a "moral" self? Does morality come from religion? From honesty? From psychological motivation? From hidden drives?

What does the text teach us about the ways in which individuals at the time in which this memoir was written could experience "their sense of being 'I'"?[47]

How does the narrating (or present) "I" regard the younger (or former) "I"? With sympathy? Embarrassment? Confusion? Shame? Pride? Annoyance?

How does the author's present position in society shape their interpretations, and thus our understanding, of the past?

How did the memoir writer form a sense of self? How was the memoir writer socialized in various contexts?[48]

Second, as Maynes, Pierce, and Laslett suggest, we might move on to questions concerning personal narrative sources in general and then questions concerning memoir as a genre itself. In so doing, we begin to raise issues about the constraints on the story. These types of questions are illustrated in box 5.2.[49]

Box 5.2: Constraints

What are the rules surrounding this memoir? What is its explicit or implicit narrative logic?

What generic considerations or models shape the choices narrators make in selecting events and details when they tell their stories?

Who is the narrator's presumed audience?

How does the intended audience inform the text itself?

How do contemporary times (that is, when the memoir was written) shape or constrain the memoir?

Why was this memoir deemed acceptable for publication? What might have made the memoir unacceptable to publishers?

As noted, memoirs take several forms, such as a coming-of-age story, conversion narrative, apology or confession, journey to freedom, or illness narrative (among others). The variety of forms gives rise to the questions in box 5.3.

Box 5.3: Forms

What form does this memoir take?

How does the form shape the message and our reaction to it?

Why did the author choose this form rather than another one?

Other questions, like those in box 5.4, challenge the assumption that first-person accounts tell what really happened, raising issues of both the vagaries of truthfulness and the basis on which authority is claimed.

Box 5.4: Truth

How would you have reacted differently had this been entirely fiction, a novel?

Does an idea of "truth" matter? Why? And to what degree? Suppose you found out that this memoir was a "fraud." Would it lose its interest for you?

How does the writer claim authority? Is it by being a witness to events? Is it by being a participant of events? Is it by the position (e.g., race, class, gender, sexual orientation) in relation to the issues raised?[50]

What kind of authority might you have believed more fully as a narrative of the issues in this memoir?

Questions about the self, the story, and the issue of verifiability would apply in many different situations. As sociologists we might ask separate sets of questions. For example, we could focus on the memoir's relationship to social norms. Philosopher Judith Butler argues that memoirs will inevitably reproduce the norms of a given society, whether social, cultural, or political norms.[51] That is, she argues, in the simple act of making oneself "legible" to one's readers, memoirs will necessarily reiterate dominant norms and values.[52] In box 5.5 I suggest questions about these issues.

Box 5.5: Norms

Do you agree with Judith Butler about the reproduction of social norms in this memoir?

How does the writer engage social norms? Are the norms conscious or unconscious? Is the actor defiant or compliant? Does the actor subvert the norms or simply play with them?[53]

Are these stories crafted to serve a particular political and social agenda? What agenda? And how is the story crafted to serve that agenda?

Oslawski-Lopez provides her students who read *I Am Malala* with discrete questions about fundamental sociological concepts such as agency, culture, social structures, social inequality, the self, and social change.[54] As illustrated in box 5.6, questions like these would be helpful in gaining sociological insight from a wide variety of texts.

Box 5.6: Concepts

How does the memoir demonstrate an interplay between individual agency and societal constraint?

What cultures did the memoir writer experience?

What social structures did the memoir writer experience, and how did those change (and with what effect)?

What types of social inequality existed or were confronted? How were wealth, power, prestige distributed (e.g., by gender)?

Does this account speak for the possibility of social change? Where might change come from?

Some Last Thoughts

In a careful review of several studies about the use of "madness / 'mental illness'" memoirs in postsecondary education, Alise de Bie, postdoctoral research fellow at McMaster University, reiterates many of the themes discussed above. Memoirs, she notes, can engage us in active learning, cultivate empathy, provide a variety of perspectives, illustrate abstract concepts, connect readers to a range of experiences outside their own, and in general help develop the sociological imagination. But de Bie sounds a note of caution that goes beyond the concern I raised above that memoirs might cause discomfort and anxiety. This additional expressed concern rests not only on the (obvious) fact that not all stories make their way into publication but also on the (equally obvious) fact that the assignment of (and reaction to) memoir inevitably involves selection, thereby ultimately privileging certain types of stories over others. De Bie thus suggests we ask a series of questions about memoir in a classroom: "What happens to the stories of [people] who come from backgrounds that students find strange, unrelatable or uninteresting?"[55] In those cases, does the use of a memoir fail to serve the goal of creating empathy?[56] What happens to the stories that do not support an instructor's pedagogical aims? Are the memoirs in a course treated as offering a "point of view" (or perspective) or a legitimate source of knowledge?

Finally, we can return to Frank's distinction and ask whether we are doing an injustice or disservice when we think *about* a story (rather than thinking *with* a story) and thereby impose theory on a narrative an author might have intended we read quite differently. In a subsequent chapter I look at a group of social scientists who, like Frank, argue just that. But first I turn to another way sociologists might think *about* memoirs—that is, to rely on them as sources of data for research projects and sociological analysis.

6

Memoirs as Data

When I submitted a prospectus for a book about family secrets to Ilene Kalish at NYU Press, she initially responded that she was "scratching [her] head a bit over [my] proposal." "I really can't think of a similar project that deals with memoir in this way," she wrote. This chapter represents a response to her puzzlement—and to anyone who might share her doubts—as I consider how sociologists can use related sets of memoirs on a given topic as the *data* for analysis.

I focus on four *book-length* studies that have sought to draw sociological conclusions by relying *exclusively* on published memoirs as their data.[1] The first of these studies, *Interpreting the Self: Two Hundred Years of American Autobiography*, by Diane Bjorklund, uses autobiographies to investigate what kind of moral "self" an individual could present at different historical moments.[2] The second, *Justifiable Conduct*, by Erich Goode, examines vocabularies of justifications in accounts of deviance.[3] The third, my research presented in *Keeping Family Secrets*, draws on both memoirs and some autobiographies to explore the consequences of extreme privacy in the post–World War II era.[4] (In what follows, when I discuss this work, I refer to myself in the third person. I do so to be consistent, and I apologize up front for the resulting awkward tone.) The last, and probably the best known, Arthur Frank's *The Wounded Storyteller*, studies vocabularies of illness.[5] Men and women are equally represented among these examples; all four authors are White. After reviewing these four projects, I consider both the advantages and disadvantages of such a data-gathering technique.

As these four studies show, in many ways the best approach to using memoirs as data is much the same as the best approach to using any other data source. After developing a research question, conducting a literature review, and ascertaining that some form of qualitative research is appropriate for the issue under investigation, we collect the necessary evidence. In some cases we will be able to make our own observations through interviews or participant observation. But, and this is the case especially if we are looking at a question about the past, we might have to rely on already available materials, like diaries, letters, memoirs, or previously collected oral histories. After gathering the data, sociologists using grounded theory will code the material, look for patterns, interpret the material, draw on and develop concepts like an "ideal type," and present the findings.[6]

But as the four examples also show, scholarship using personal narratives requires a specific way of thinking and a specific mode of analysis. First, it builds from the subjective perceptions individuals have about social phenomena and from the ways in which they write about their own experiences.[7] Because the subjective is so central here, researchers using these sources must be particularly attentive to the constraints on the form and content of the available material with respect to issues like the reliability of memory, the intrusion of creative elements, the presumed audience, the historical context, and the publishing industry. They also need to be aware of the distinctive conventions for the particular genre known as memoir at a particular moment in time as well as the reasons why some rather than other narratives become public.[8] In addition, scholars using this kind of data have to address the issue of representativeness, an issue that might otherwise be solved by drawing a random sample: How well do the writers of published memoirs represent the population from which they are drawn? What limits might we have to impose on interpretation stemming from a lack of representativeness? What other conclusions could we draw if more—or different— sources were available?

Four Examples

Diane Bjorklund, Interpreting the Self: Two Hundred Years of American Autobiography

Diane Bjorklund's book relies on reading and coding 110 autobiographies written in the United States between 1800 and 1980 to discover how the presentation of the self changed over time.[9] Bjorklund selected these autobiographies for what she refers to as a "judgement sample" from two annotated bibliographies, making sure she had at least five manuscripts from each decade in her time period.[10]

Employing the sociological concept of an ideal type, and without claims that the types she discovers either are "comprehensive [or] encompass the diversity found among autobiographies," she suggests four common varieties of representation of a self, spanning four different historical moments.[11] Religious autobiographies, prevalent in the nineteenth century, portray a self who wrestles with an innately corrupt human nature and is "saved" by religious conversion. A competing model, also found in the nineteenth century, links the promise of evolutionary theory to an optimistic notion of self-discovery, producing a self who, with sufficient character and willpower, could take control of their own fate. As psychology becomes prominent at the turn of the twentieth century, autobiographers have access to new concepts and theories through which they might account for their own actions. Those with a psychological bent look for the ways in which emotions, instincts, and drives could explain human behavior. Bjorklund then reports on the emergence of a self that recognizes and responds to the influence of society, overlapping with the other three types in time but becoming more prominent in the latter part of the twentieth century.

In identifying these types of selves, Bjorklund makes a broad argument about the significance of the "larger cultural discourse [that] furnishes not only ideas about the nature of selfhood but also evaluative standards for model selves and model lives."[12] At each of the four moments she identifies, autobiographers grapple with the moral issue of how much responsibility they could take for the way they conducted their lives. The different answers they give respond to changing moral standards. In short, her historical approach vividly demonstrates that what can count as virtuous behavior—including the virtue of honesty— has changed over time.

Bjorklund probes autobiographies less for their narrative quality— the how and why of the prose within them—than for the what—the content of what the writers are saying (or not saying), and especially for what they are saying (or not saying) about how best to justify individual behavior. In an early chapter, Bjorklund emphasizes that the writing of an autobiography is a *social* act, "both as part of a 'community of discourse'; and as a type of social interaction in which one tries to influence others."[13] Although autobiographers are "constrained by cultural vocabularies of the self," they are "not simply passive reflectors of such vocabularies: they select, interpret, and adapt shared cultural ideas to interpret their lives and to engage in artful self-presentation."[14] Thus, in Bjorklund's analysis, the autobiographical writer stands somewhere in that murky place (where, ultimately, we all stand) between having free will and being socially determined. We cannot make sense of the autobiographies she references (or any autobiographies) unless we understand the context that constrains *and* furnishes vocabulary. Nor can we read autobiographies without granting room for creativity.

From start to finish this is a serious sociological work. Bjorklund asks a set of questions central not just to the sociological study of autobiography but also to the sociological study of the self: "How has the way in which American autobiographers construct (present) their lives changed over time? What vocabularies of the self do they deploy? How do they use shared cultural understandings of the self and historical-situation constraints of self-presentation to write their lives as narratives?"[15] And in her response, the distinctive aspects of memoir—that they are subjective and unreliable—become the focus of analysis. That is, Bjorklund interrogates the chosen frames for the presentation of a moral self, not the veracity of any given narrative.

Erich Goode, Justifiable Conduct: Self-Vindication in Memoir

Erich Goode writes that his research focus is "the process by which autobiographers and memoirists explain, justify, exculpate, excuse, and warrant" behavior that is defined as deviant in their social worlds.[16] He differs from Bjorklund in several ways. First, he is not at all interested in how these justifications change over time. Second, he does not carefully randomize his selection. His selection process, he admits himself, is "somewhat haphazard," drawing from "American memoirs" and on "the fairly well-known over the obscure and the fairly recent over older samples."[17] Third, he organizes his analysis by types of "deviance" that cut across time rather than change over time. These types include criminal behavior, substance abuse, sexual transgressions, and political transgressions. For each case he draws on several examples as he searches for common themes.

Different as he might be from Bjorklund, Goode also asks questions that are sociological. His queries emerge from the literature of the social construction of deviance as presented by scholars like Howard Becker and from the literature on accounts of deviant behavior as presented by scholars like Gresham Sykes and David Matza.[18] What language, he inquires, is available to those who engage in deviance, and does the language differ by the "content" of the deviance? That is, he is interested in how deviants write about their deviant acts; these writings, he notes, are "put together in specific ways to convey specific meanings." They thus become the data that demand sociological investigation and understanding.[19]

Although Goode explores differences within deviance categories and between different forms of deviance, he also finds commonalities among the authors with respect to the demands made on their readers: "Almost contradictorily, they want to excite, impress, surprise, and even shock them, yet at the same time they want to create a verbal cushion that reassures them that they are not a shoddy, deplorable species of humanity. They seem to beg us for our love in spite of their sins."[20] In his conclusion, Goode argues that the "deviant" is not different from any other member of the human community, that we all "are always looking over our shoulders at what others think of who we are, what we do, and how we feel."[21] And we all want to look good in the eyes of others.

Margaret K. Nelson, Keeping Family Secrets: Shame and Silence in Memoirs from the 1950s

By way of contrast to both Bjorklund and Goode, Margaret Nelson's scholarship uses memoirs to highlight a distinctive set of issues during a single historical period.[22] Drawing on over a hundred fifty memoirs about growing up in the United States in the post–World War II era, Nelson explores how the writers presented the reasons for, and their perceptions of the consequences of, keeping four different secrets from other family members and especially from those outside the family. The four secrets include having same-sex sexual attractions as boys, being young, pregnant, and unwed, having an institutionalized sibling, and living with parents who were members of the Communist Party. Nelson also examines the family dynamics that ensued when people discovered that parents had kept secrets from them during their childhoods. These secrets include learning that one or both parents were Jewish and learning that they had been adopted (or conceived outside of the marital union).

Like Bjorklund and Goode, Nelson relies on the grounded theory approach, first grouping the available memoirs into the categories of the kind of secret under investigation and then looking for shared elements across the various narratives. And as is the case for both Bjorklund and Goode, Nelson's questions are sociological. Her work derives from an interest in the intersection of the historical and the biographical. She asks how the social constraints of the 1940s and 1950s created a world in which certain behaviors had to remain secret. And she asks how keeping secrets shaped family life. The analysis thus moves from broad to narrow, from the political, social, and cultural context to the attitudes and emotions of individual family members. It also moves back out again: she argues that when the members of a family kept secrets from each other and from the world outside the home, secrecy became a social way of life.

Nelson briefly acknowledges a possible constraint on the narrative arc of these memoirs. Most end on a redemptive note. Ultimately, almost all authors forgive the harm they believe their parents inflicted; they come to be sympathetic about why their parents acted as they did. We can easily imagine other endings such as persistent anger and permanent alienation; we can also easily imagine that these might not have been acceptable to the editors who were advising these writers or to the publishers accepting and promoting the work. Moreover, these authors might well have been constructing a compassionate self, presenting themselves as "survivors" who have overcome the harms done to them and gracious enough to forgive those who had done them harm. But unlike Bjorklund, Nelson's interest is not in the self per se; rather, it is in the way that secrets shape interactions within a family.

Arthur Frank, The Wounded Storyteller: Body, Illness, and Ethics

Although discussed last, Arthur Frank's book was written before the other examples included here. In his hands the narrative form is the subject itself. Frank wants to know what types of stories the culture makes available to speak about the experience of serious illness.[23] That is, he intends not to tell us how we experience illness but to describe the ways in which people represent their illnesses to others. In so doing, he identifies the three kinds of narrative he believes tell the story of suffering from illness in postmodern times: restitution, chaos, and quest narratives.

The restitution narrative has a basic storyline: "Yesterday I was healthy, today I'm sick, but tomorrow I'll be healthy again."[24] Frank says this is "the culturally preferred narrative because it "attempt[s] to outdistance mortality by rendering illness transitory." Frank next outlines chaos as a competing narrative: chaos is the "opposite of restitution," with a plot that "imagines life never getting better."[25] In a sense, Frank writes, these stories are not fully narratives because they do not tell of a "sequence of events connected to each other through time." And unlike restitution narratives, chaos stories provoke anxiety; they pull people into "the undertow of illness and the disasters that attend it."[26] Finally, quest stories, a third narrative form, "meet suffering head on: they accept illness and seek to *use* it."

If for Bjorklund and Goode the stories contained in autobiographical writing represent a social self within the cultural vocabulary of a given time, for Frank illness narratives are neither about a self nor about the body. These, he contends, are stories told *through* the body. Thus, telling the story of one's illness is both performative and transformative. The storyteller "bears witness to that suffering and reflects on its meaning in the context of [their] life."[27] Ultimately Frank is interested in the "ethical significance of patient testimony—in relation to, though not contained by, medical practice." In fact, what Frank refers to as "narrative ethics" (with its notion of thinking with, not about, a story, as discussed in chapter 5) might preclude our doing just what I am doing here as I hold the stories he tells to the harsh light of analysis.

Evaluating This Method

Taken together these four studies help us identify some of the advantages—and the related disadvantages—of using memoirs as data. In previous chapters I raised some of the reasons for looking at memoirs—from the perspective of their sociocultural importance and the contemporary diverse group of people who contribute to the genre. I noted that memoirs might replicate hegemonic ideas but might also resist those very ideas. And I suggested that when building sociology from the evidence embedded in memoirs we need to be especially attentive to their covert messages. I reiterate some of these issues here and raise some new ones.

Subjectivity

As the discussion to this point has made clear, the subjectivity that is often viewed as a problem in research is precisely the reason memoirs can be so valuable for sociological analysis. As Maynes, Pierce, and Laslett argue, that subjectivity "opens space for new understandings of the relationship between the individual and the social."[28] Of course, we know nothing about how honestly individuals write any more than we know anything about how honestly they respond to the questions asked in interviews and surveys. We can, however, safely assume that memoirists want to present themselves in the best light—or in the light they think will most appeal to readers. And sometimes this biased presentation provides precisely the data that social scientists might want, as is the case for both Bjorklund and Goode: Bjorklund wants to know how individuals at different points of time came to think of themselves as moral; Goode wants to understand the vocabularies available as justifications for deviant acts.

Access

Because published memoirs already exist in the world, they not only provide readily available forms of data but also can offer access to voices we might otherwise be unable to reach, especially if we are short on resources or investigating something in the past. Bjorklund wanted to know how ideas of the self changed over time, starting as early as 1800 and continuing to the present. Clearly, she could not have interviewed appropriate subjects: they were no longer alive. Nor would these individuals necessarily have left letters and diaries; in any case, those documents would not have illustrated the *public* presentation of a self. But she had access to the writings of individuals who lived over two centuries ago. And those individuals had a particular interest in presenting themselves as "moral," as commendable, as decent in the lexicon of the times. Fortunately for Bjorklund they enacted that interest by speaking to their peers through the social act of writing and publishing autobiographies. Similarly, Goode had access to public presentations by "deviants" interested in accounting for themselves in an exculpatory manner. These same individuals might have presented themselves quite differently in other settings (e.g., when pleading guilty or not guilty in court). Because Nelson's "subjects" were more likely than Bjorklund's to still be alive (although many were not), she might have interviewed them had she been able to locate/identify people willing to speak with her about childhoods consumed by keeping secrets. But it is hard to imagine how she would have framed a call for respondents, where she would have advertised that call, and who—if anyone—would have agreed to tell their stories. The same issue of identifying and locating appropriate subjects would have arisen for Frank.

In short, memoirs can solve problems of access to vital informants. Moreover, it is possible to find memoirs on a broad range of specific topics. And sets of memoirs on a single topic are easy to find by going to booksellers' web pages, sites for readers, or the home pages of special interest groups. For example, if you are interested in issues of adoption, you need merely ask Amazon for its suggestions; Goodreads will also provide you with a list (along with ratings by readers); and the American Adoptions site offers its own list of "20 of the Best Adoptee Books Out There."[29] Of course I am not endorsing the pursuit of a topic like adoption only through or even primarily through memoir. But I am suggesting that memoirs exist as a vehicle with which to seek to understand major aspects of that experience.

Sadly, the range of content of memoirs is not endless, and there may be no memoirs or too few to enable us to research every subject of sociological interest.[30] Moreover, any level of availability rests on a publisher's interest in buying a manuscript; that interest, in turn, rests on what is likely to sell. As noted repeatedly, not all stories will appear in the public domain at a given point in time. To take just one example, none of the boys with same-sex desires who wrote the memoirs Nelson used in her analysis of family secrets felt comfortable sharing their innermost thoughts with their parents or siblings during their childhoods. If a different set of individuals existed, their stories of openness and acceptance would have provided less dramatic tension and publishers might well have rejected their work. And among those published, almost all the memoirists forgave their parents; publishers might not have found unforgiving anger equally attractive.

Variety

For centuries now both White men and White women have written memoirs. Increasingly today, not only White people but members of marginalized communities write memoirs. People from all over the country, with different religious affiliations (or none) and varied immigrant statuses, write memoirs. Young people write them as do those who are middle aged or older. Those who are able-bodied write memoirs, as do those whose physical or mental disabilities make their lives more challenging. LGBTQ+ people write memoirs as well as those who are straight and cisgender. Indeed, now that self-publication is a more prevalent possibility, the range of people who might write memoirs is probably broader today than it has ever been.

But the range is not endless. Quite simply, some people cannot write their own stories (or even find a ghostwriter to help them): these include the still uneducated, those for whom the daily grind leaves no time to reflect on, much less record, their thoughts, those who lack or are denied the wherewithal to write (including the unsheltered, those living in mental institutions, and those who are incarcerated), and those whose illnesses and disabilities preclude the achievement of the type of clearheadedness memoir writing requires. And it might be difficult to know the reasons for and therefore interpret the absence of material from specific groups. To take another example from Nelson's *Keeping Family Secrets*, no woman of color wrote about her experience of unwed pregnancy and having been compelled to give up her baby for adoption. How could we know what this meant? That no women of color were in that precise situation? That women of color were more reluctant to reveal this aspect of their life? Or was there some other, entirely different reason?

Representativeness matters for how we make sense of specific topics. Cindee Calton, a disability scholar, interrogates the memoirs of nine parents of children with disabilities to understand how they gained access to the resources that enabled independent living for their children.[31] The authors were all members of the middle or upper middle class. As a result, she writes, they were able "to draw on significant resource of time, money, and social connection to cope with the extra needs of their children." Similarly, Allison C. Carey, also a disability scholar, bases her article on fourteen memoirs published by parents of children with intellectual disabilities.[32] All were "written by parents who were financially secure, well educated, white, living in nuclear families (at least when the children were born, although some later divorced), and living in wealthy, democratic nations." In short, those parents had resources "that allowed them to access, assess, and criticize the systems with which they interacted and to use memoir as a form of activism." As a group, however, Carey notes, even when they recognized "their own privileged position, more often than not they failed to consider how race, class, education, and their position as nondisabled parents affected their experiences and perspectives." More generally, we might ask who writes—and importantly who does *not* write—about a range of issues. Does *anyone* write about having abused a child? Do bigamists report their deceptions?

Although representative matters, we may have no idea of the *universe* of memoirs we might draw from. Quite simply, we cannot sample our respondents. Frank makes this point in *The Wounded Storyteller* when he says he could not find a way to make his sample representative "both because there is so much written and because illness figures variously in many different memoirs." Further, he adds, "What counts as an illness story is by no means clear."[33]

Issues of representativeness rise in another way when we consider that people have usually overcome the trials and tribulations that constitute the meat of so many memoirs—abuse, illness, captivity, poverty, anorexia—when they have the time and space to write. Tara Westover, author of the highly acclaimed *Educated*, grew up in dismal poverty and suffered daily abuse.[34] By the time she wrote her memoir she had received a degree from the University of Cambridge. Mary Childers, author of *Welfare Brat*, also had a doctorate in English literature and worked as a consultant who mediated conflict and provided discrimination-prevention training for higher education.[35] J. D. Vance, author of *Hillbilly Elegy*, earned a law degree from Yale University (and is, at the time of this writing, the Republican vice presidential candidate).[36] These eventual achievements matter for at least two reasons.

First, they demand some accounting for success. Vance would want us to believe that his achievements rest on the exercise of agency (as well as his own intelligence) and that, therefore, others also could leave their childhoods in Appalachia behind. Similar attitudes toward individual agency are often found in stories of addiction written by those who believe they have overcome that affliction (e.g., Matthew Perry) rather than by those who know they are still in its thrall.[37] Westover and Childers both suggest that academic aptitude can make a crucial difference in the achievement of upward mobility. As such, they offer little hope not only for those whose ability is neither noticed nor nurtured but also for those who—for whatever reason—find education challenging or even entirely beyond their reach.

Second, success changes one's perspective. People adapt to, and acquire the orientation of, the social class position they have achieved, shedding their previous behaviors and attitudes. Adrian J. Rivera, an editorial assistant with *Times* Opinion, writes as much in his essay, "I Am Mourning the Loss of Something I Loved: McNuggets."[38] His "social education" (like Vance's) began when he went to Yale where he found himself "listening to some classmates chatting about ice cream, home-made with fresh strawberries. They went on about how singular and spectacular it was, about how much they loved it. I'd never eaten ice cream made with fresh strawberries, had never eaten homemade ice cream." When he joined the conversation with a comment about liking "the flavor of artificial strawberry ice cream," his classmates sent looks suggesting that he was an "alien." Although for some time he clung to the tastes of his childhood, and although he still mourns the time when "eating a McNugget could still transport [him] to a time of warmth and love and safety," eventually he abandoned his tastes because now he knew "better."[39]

They Exist without Us

Even with these limitations on who writes memoirs and what they repre-sent by way of social positions, an enormous number of memoirs do exist and cover a wide range of topics about the past and the present. More-over, they have the benefit of existing without our influence. As social scientists became increasingly reflexive about their research methods in the second half of the twentieth century, they began to acknowledge that they had a profound influence on the form and content of the data collected through such methods as questionnaires, interviews, and par-ticipant observation. To contextualize those influences, some began to share their biases, their perceptions of how their characteristics might have shaped the questions they asked, the interview process, and the interactions on which they based their observations. But we have no part in the production of memoirs; quite simply, we do not bring them into existence.

Of course, as noted repeatedly, many factors constrain these writings. In fact, for some subjects—as for the issues addressed by Bjorklund, Goode, and Frank—that constraint constitutes a key part of the analysis itself: the writers can draw on only the available vocabularies with which to present themselves and their concerns. But for the most part the sociologists themselves are out of the picture, that is, until they begin to select which memoirs to use and how to approach them for analysis. Then, of course, their social characteristics and personal biases will become relevant, and they should be transparent about those characteristics and those biases. But, again, there is nothing unique here: as Pamela Cotterill and Gayle Letherby note, "All research contains elements of autobiography and biography, both intellectual and personal."[40]

Yet there is a downside here too in the fact that memoirs exist as published documents. The "finished" quality of memoirs limits our ability to interrogate "informants": we cannot probe, we cannot follow up, we cannot ask about issues of concern *not* addressed in the memoir itself. This makes a reliance on memoirs like a reliance on letters or diaries quite different from a reliance on sources that allow researchers to add new questions. "Tell me more about that," I often asked as an interviewer; "Can you explain what you mean?" Sometimes, interviewers return many times (and sometimes over a period of many years) to understand experiences of growth and transformation.[41] Published memoirs give us just one chance at understanding an "informant's" perspective or point of view. We cannot ask the authors how accurately they think they remembered the events in the stories they tell or even how accurately they are reporting their life experiences. We cannot return to the authors a year later and ask them if they still feel the same way about a particular event or whether their attitudes have changed.

They Are Available to Others

Unless scholars make available the raw data they use for their analyses (the recordings or transcripts of interviews; the letters hidden in obscure archives; the data files), the reader must trust the scholar to have interpreted and presented the material accurately. Published memoirs, however, open the scholar's assertions to reanalysis and reinterpretation. Anyone can buy the books we included, look for the quotes we used, assess that usage, and draw their own conclusions. That awareness might help rein us in. If they are still alive, the people we have written about also might protest, argue, and offer their own point of view. They can talk back. That is the challenge of giving up the practice of anonymizing our "subjects." In addition, on a more positive note, when we name our "subjects," we connect to the "real" world and its ongoing history.

There is still another benefit. In the interest of assuring anonymity to their subjects, sociologists might change some details of a given individual or on occasion combine several examples and present them as a single person. We might consider these changes incidental—or at least hope that they are incidental, that they do not alter the import of what we are saying. But of course as sociologists we believe the particularities of people's lives matter and that even seemingly trivial details, like the city in which they grew up, the occupation they hold, the name with which they faced the world, the color of their hair, and the shape of their bodies, all leave an imprint on a person's life. When we assign pseudonyms or alter these details, we do violence to veracity. Dena Davis, a law professor, makes this point in a discussion of her case studies of people with illnesses: "The standard often set as the ideal is that the patient herself, reading the account, would not recognize herself in it. But when I began to describe the cases on paper, I realized that I was confronting a powerful paradox: the very details that needed to be falsified were just those that gave the cases their integrity and usefulness. Here I was with four narratives, rather enjoying the prospect of playing with the details, inventing some names, adding a little embroidery, fulfilling my novelistic fantasies. But what could be changed?" Davis ends up advocating for making better use of "nonfiction accounts of . . . journeys through illness, death and disability."[42] In memoirs the authors supply the "thick description"; we need not make it up. But, as mentioned already, we may not find the description "thick" enough and we cannot ask for more.

These days institutional review boards protect research subjects. They constrain access to vulnerable populations; they check to ensure questions are not too intrusive; they make certain that the research process does not expose individual identities. By drawing on published memoirs, sociologists circumvent these constraints. The research "subjects" have already exposed themselves. At the same time, we might consider whether ethical issues still arise in using memoirs for purposes that extend far beyond those the authors intended.[43] And we might ask whether it is "fair" to impose contemporary standards of conduct and disclosure on those who acted and wrote within different sets of constraints. As we saw with memoirs written by sociologists, some revealed themselves to be oblivious to their own privileges and some resisted new ways of evaluating their scholarship. Should we judge them by our notions of what constitutes appropriate behavior today?

In the next chapter I look at those who draw on their own experiences rather than the experiences of others as the foundation for their scholarship and, among them, at those who believe that an analytic framework is entirely the wrong way to read and write about those experiences. I also slightly shift my voice; I am more attentive in the next chapter to issues that might be of significant to my colleagues than to students (such as finding a way through differently labeled but similar pieces of scholarship or through debates within a field). The subsequent chapter addresses college teachers who might want to assign personal writing in their classrooms.

PART IV

Teaching Personal Writing

7

Autoethnography

In his retirement Fred Pincus, a sociologist who taught courses on race relations and diversity for over four decades at the University of Maryland Baltimore County, chose to write a memoir (in part about growing up with parents who were communists). In an essay about his career included in Rosalyn Darling and Peter Stein's *Journeys in Sociology: From First Encounters to Fulfilling Retirements*, he describes what happened when a colleague invited him to speak about this memoir for her class on "the sociology of the life cycle." The students, who had read his draft chapters about his childhood and years in college, asked numerous questions. In response, Pincus writes, "I found myself talking less about sociological concepts and more about me." The colleague, Pincus continues, then "informed the class that my chapters were a good example of a methodology called autoethnography." Pincus was surprised: "Huh? I thought. What's that? I never heard of autoethnography. I'm writing a memoir." Curious, Pincus decided to do "a little reading about autoethnography, wondering if this would legitimate [his] memoir in the eyes of social scientists." "This methodology," he discovered, "is defined as connecting personal experiences to the larger social, political, and economic context." He also discovered long methodological pieces describing this approach; even the "Wikipedia entry on autoethnography, . . . was ten single-spaced pages with over forty references." Reluctant to "enter a new academic field," Pincus eventually became dismissive: "If they want to describe [my writing] as autoethnographical," he wrote, "so be it. . . . I can be both a writer and a sociologist. I no longer have to worry about what is scholarly and what is literary. I'm retired."[1]

Small wonder that Pincus got overwhelmed. The number of overlapping terms preceding and surrounding what is known today as auto-ethnography is astounding. So too are the number of books and articles purporting to define the term and explain it as *method*. A little terminological history might help orient us.

Terminological History

In an essay written in 1988 Robert K. Merton defines "sociological autobiography" as an approach that "utilizes sociological perspectives, ideas, concepts, findings, and analytical procedures to construct and to interpret the narrative text that purports to tell one's own history within the context of the larger history of one's times."[2] Merton thus puts the emphasis on how authors applied the tools and concepts of sociology to both build and make sense of their own life histories. Ultimately, for Merton, the goal is enrichment of the field of sociology by applying its concepts to understanding the development of an individual life and the intellectual work that life produced. And, as we will see in the next chapter, this approach can be helpful in learning sociology.

That same year, Paul Higgins and John Johnson collected essays they referred to as "personal sociology" as an example of a reflexive approach. Those who practice personal sociology, they write, "view their own lives in the ways that most now view the lives of others." They continue, "There are no subjects to be studied, but people to be understood—others and oneself. The personal sociologists' experiences give rise to concerns that transcend those immediate experiences."[3] And they provide examples of how personal sociology develops: "The sociologist who is a musician seeks to understand art worlds.[4] The ex-con turned sociologist investigates the transformation of prisons and prison reform.[5] The sociologist, involved in the women's movement and a student of organizations, examines men and women in corporations."[6] Higgins and Johnson also defend this approach against the charge that they—and others writing in the same vein—are simply self-absorbed narcissists or "navel gazers." Rather, Higgins and Johnson claim that personal sociology uses an individual sociologist's life as the starting point of sociological analysis, moving out from the individual to the broader context in which that person is embedded rather than, as Merton suggests sociological autobiography would do, moving inward by applying sociological concepts to the understanding of an individual's personal history.[7]

Two years later, in 1990, Norman L. Friedman, in an article published in the *American Sociologist*, reverses the terms of sociological autobiography, now referring to something he calls "autobiographical sociology" in a way that is akin to what Higgins and Johnson had called personal sociology. He defines autobiographical sociology as an endeavor in which "a sociologist probes one or more past personal experiences as a way of identifying and analyzing something sociologically relevant." This approach, he continues, "contained elements of ethnography because of its emphasis on participant observation and autobiography." To distinguish autobiographical sociology from other approaches to which he believed it was "similar" and "related" (including "opportunistic research, auto-ethnography, experiential analysis, complete member research, personal sociology, postmodern ethnography, and 'conventional covert worker ethnography'"), Friedman claims that his approach relied on a greater emphasis on the "past-time" or "autobiographical element." As such, he argues that autobiographical sociology "highlights the sociological insights gained through autobiographical experiences and information" rather than applying sociological insights to account for the dynamics or progression of one's life.[8] Autobiographical sociology, in Friedman's view, like personal sociology, uses the sociologist's experiences to build concepts; if it is in any way different from what Higgins and Johnson called personal sociology, it is because of its focus on the past.[9]

To add to the confusion, in 1996 Arthur B. Shostak, in an edited collection he calls *Private Sociology: Unsparing Reflections, Uncommon Gains*, uses the term "autobiographical sociology" to refer to what Merton had called sociological autobiography. But he condemns sociological autobiography (or autobiographical sociology) as collected in Riley's set of essays, *Sociological Lives: Social Change and the Life Course*, for being too "prim and proper."[10] Rather than avoiding complicated or painful issues, *private* sociology, Shostak writes, is "the study of that which we hesitate to tell." He adds that private sociology reads more like memoir than like autobiography: private sociology "replaces the wide-angle lens with a close-up focus on some selected aspects of the tale."[11] Curiously, for sociologists, neither Shostak in his writing about private sociology nor Friedman in his writing about personal sociology acknowledges that as norms about disclosure change, what might be regarded as private or personal one day might be food for TikTok or Instagram the next.

Recently, the derisive term "me-search" (alternatively "MeSearch" or "mesearch") has appeared to describe scholarship motivated by both its relevance to the individual conducting the research and an understanding that the topic has been understudied. The work of lesbians studying lesbian motherhood, Jamaicans studying life in Jamaica, and people with disabilities studying stigma might all be identified as "me-search" *if* the researchers make known their identity as a member of the group under investigation or draw on their own firsthand experience with the material. Not only is the term to describe this approach derisive, but this approach exposes scholars to the accusation that their research is biased and that they are engaged in a narcissistic project of self-discovery.[12] In response to these charges, scholars insist on the excitement, significance, and expertise that this research might have. At the American Sociological Association 2023 annual meetings, Angela Elena Fillingim of San Francisco State University presided over a panel titled "Reflections on the Educative Power of 'Mesearch.'" The description suggests that the panelists would come to the defense of this approach: "Although often derided, so-called 'mesearch' is a vital source of and motivation for sociological knowledge. How might embracing, rather than distancing, our research from our personal biographies and community relations improve, strengthen, and challenge sociological knowledge? How might this important source of knowledge matter across methodological divides?"[13]

Even greater conceptual and terminological troubles loom because a subset of writers—some of them sociologists, many of them not—claim what they term "autoethnography" not as something in the same family as sociological autobiography, autobiographical sociology, personal, private sociology, or even (on occasion) "me-search," but as a form in and of itself with its own origins and its own method.

Originally, the term "autoethnography" arose when some anthropologists promoted it as a way to put the anthropologists themselves back in. These scholars wanted to show that where individual anthropologists came from, their status in relation to the people they studied, and their own personal characteristics all shaped what they could learn and what they could write. Considering these critiques, some anthropologists asserted that the best (and even the only valid or legitimate) ethnography was autoethnography, defined as a way of studying one's own people.[14]

Some sociologists, similarly, demanded—or asked politely—that their colleagues do the same. All sociologists, they insisted, should acknowledge that their personal characteristics shaped their observations. As did some anthropologists, occasionally sociologists also claimed the only worthwhile study was of oneself as located in a particular social and cultural context. Ronald J. Berger and Richard Quinney, for example, see autoethnography as emerging as an "identifiable research strategy" at a time of "epistemological reappraisal in the social sciences."[15] Simultaneously, other scholars, bemoaning the jargon and general obscurity of most academic texts, asked for writing that was more creative, more literary, and more accessible.[16] Both the epistemological reappraisal and the shift in writing strategy were elements of the narrative turn discussed in chapter 1. Since then, a broad swath of social scientists, some eagerly, some grudgingly, in fields extending beyond sociology and anthropology to include communication studies,[17] psychology,[18] and education studies, have claimed that autoethnography is an appropriate method to solve a host of issues surrounding representation and writing.[19]

Over time, and however modest it was in its initial claims, the approach known as autoethnography has entirely eclipsed any of the other approaches mentioned above. For the ten-year period from 2012 to 2022, Google Scholar returned 39 references for the term "private sociology," 69 for "autobiographical sociology," 126 for "personal sociology," 203 for "sociological autobiography," 3,740 for "me-search" (many of which have nothing to do with sociology), and the walloping number of over 33,200 for "autoethnography" (again, many of which have nothing to do with sociology).

So what is autoethnography—and what are its claims? That, it turns out, depends on whom you ask, and perhaps even depends on when you ask them.[20]

Autoethnography Defined and Debated

In a recent textbook, communications professor Christopher Poulos acknowledges varying definitions of the field of autoethnography, within which a core of three elements exists: writing (*graphia*) about the self (*auto*), as situated within a social group, culture, or people (*ethnos*).[21] Within this core battles rage. As spelled out in a series of essays in the *Journal of Contemporary Ethnography* in 2006, autoethnographers disagreed wildly then—as they still do today—about just how much overt analysis an autoethnography must—or even should—include.

Analytic Ethnography

At one end Leon Anderson makes a case for what he calls analytic ethnography as a methodological approach using an individual's life experience as the data that can explicate larger social processes (much as Shostak described private sociology). Anderson lays out its key features to include "1) complete member researcher (CMR) status, 2) analytic reflexivity, 3) narrative visibility of the researcher's self, 4) dialogue with informants beyond the self, and 5) commitment to theoretical analysis."[22] As defined, this approach focuses on the fieldwork experience while treating the personal experience as "tangential," expects coding and thematic analysis, and in general adheres to the same writing practices in structure and language as do other disciplinary products.[23]

In sum, *analytic* autoethnography, its proponents claim, must go beyond description, beyond simply "capturing 'what is going on.'" It requires analysis, by which Leon Anderson means "a broad set of data-transcending practices" directed toward "theoretical development, refinement, and extension."[24] Anderson cites as an example of what he expects of this approach Robert Murphy's 2001 book *The Body Silent: The Different World of the Disabled*, in which an anthropologist uses his experience of paralysis to explore the damage inflicted by social attitudes toward disability and the ways in which disability shapes one's identity, bonds with others, and social standing.[25] As a more contemporary example, we might turn to any of a number of books or shorter essays including Robert Courtney Smith's "analytic autoethnography" of the "variable social identity construction" of his father over the course of the two years before he died of Alzheimer's disease.[26] In this piece, Smith draws on his own memories as well as those of family members to create what he calls "collective triangulated accounts of a shared history"; he also explicitly refers to theories of the self and of Alzheimer's disease as a means to interpret that shared history.[27] More recently, although he calls it "personal sociology," Jeffrey Nash offers a series of linked essays that analyze a variety of topics building on "participant observation in the social domain being described."[28] Three essays address how Nash's gender intersects with his other identities, two focus on "interconnections among humor, race, class, disability, and gender," and three explore his social activism in social contexts.

In the eyes of its practitioners, the form of autoethnography prescribed by Anderson adheres closely to traditional ethnography. But its advocates argue that analytic autoethnography has virtues that supersede that approach and that might make this form especially appropriate for use in a sociology course. Writing from the perspective of being an insider, proponents explain, not only facilitates access to data but ensures that the researcher understands the meanings known only to insiders. Moreover, as is the case for memoirs themselves, the inclusion of the personal often makes the research especially engaging. From the perspective of analysis, this type of autoethnography offers what its adherents refer to as rich opportunities to pursue the connections between individual biography and social structure. It thus helps achieve the promise of sociology as laid out by C. Wright Mills. Of course—and Anderson acknowledges this—autoethnography does have limits: not all scholars have research interests deeply entwined with their personal lives; not everyone wants to look inward to themselves for research material.

In the 2006 special issue of the *Journal of Contemporary Ethnography* devoted to autoethnography, Paul Atkinson essentially sides with Anderson, claiming that "the goals of analysis and theorizing are too often lost to sight in contemporary fashions for subjective and evocative ethnographic work."[29] Kevin Vryan also aligns his orientation with that of Anderson even as he takes issue with some elements of Anderson's argument.[30] The same is true of Kathy Charmaz, who questions whether "the name *autoethnography* will stretch to include the kinds of ethnographic works that Anderson would like to place under it." She asks, "Would Clinton Sanders, David Karp, and Loic Wacquant recognize themselves as autoethnographers, albeit of the analytic type? Would they want to be so named?"[31]

Evocative Autoethnography

At the other end, another group of autoethnographers have nothing but contempt for Anderson's notion of what makes for good autoethnography. Norm Denzin in the same *Journal of Contemporary Ethnography* issue puts forth an alternative position and provides an alternative example of autoethnography in the form of what he calls a "dramatic, performance poetic . . . that includes excerpts from personal histories, official and unofficial government documents, scholarly articles, and popular culture texts" but no theoretical analysis of those items.[32]

Two key figures in writing about autoethnography, Art Bochner and Carolyn Ellis, also want none of Anderson's analytic approach. In their book, *Evocative Autoethnography: Writing Lives and Telling Stories*, they insist that Anderson, "wants to take what is unruly, vulnerable, rebellious, and creative about autoethnography and bring it back under the control of reason and analysis."[33] They complain that Anderson and his ilk "eschew both the 'art' of 'he(art)-ful' autoethnography and its value-centeredness." And they continue with contempt, arguing that the analytic autoethnographers "cling to the traditional goals of generalization, distanced analysis, and theory-building, directing their work mainly to other scholars . . . [but] show little interest in the kind of understanding aroused by evoking emotional reactions that inspire readers to reflect critically on their own lives and turn those reflections into actions."[34]

In the place of analytic autoethnography, Bochner and Ellis propose "evocative or emotional ethnography," with its focus on feeling, artfulness, and storytelling that we perceive as being both "true and real." In multiple publications they define their approach as an "autobiographical genre of writing and research that displays multiple layers of consciousness, connecting the personal to the cultural." They are open about form, allowing the use of "short stories, poetry, fiction, novels, photographic essays, personal essays, journals, fragmented and layered writing, and social science prose."[35]

Bochner and Ellis further explain and illustrate their goals in a manuscript that follows the form of a workshop. They draw on two examples throughout. One, a short piece by Ellis, titled "Maternal Connections," describes the care Ellis gave her mother when the latter was dying. No overt sociological analysis appears. Readers might well be touched, moved, and drawn to reflect on their own experiences. But as is the case for the many memoirs discussed in chapter 3, for the piece to be a useful tool for learning sociology, readers must do the analytical work themselves. The second piece, Bochner's short story "Bird on Wire," consists of an imaginary conversation between Bochner and his deceased father. In discussing this piece with his imaginary (and occasionally imagined to be confrontational) students, Bochner reminds them of Frank's distinction between thinking *with* and thinking *about* a story and advocates only the former.[36] Moreover the question of whether or not it is "true" becomes grist for a lesson about the difference between works of fiction (as a novelist would write) and works of "imagination" (as an autoethnographer would write) in which the author is not free to make things up but is bound, Bochner suggests, "by the particular events that I recall having occurred in my life."[37]

Carolyn Ellis's early work, *Final Negotiations: A Story of Love, Loss, and Chronic Illness*, tells the story of her relationship with her professor and lover, sociologist Gene Weinstein, during the years he became increasingly ill from COPD. Ellis also ends the story with analytic chapters. However, she leaves the narrative untouched by the framing analysis.[38] More recently Laurel Richardson's *Story of a Marriage* provides another book-length example. Richardson narrates the end of her husband's life as he endured a particularly cruel form of dementia in the hope "that those who have suffered from Lewy Body as caregivers, family, or friends of those afflicted with the disease will find in this book someone who has walked in your shoes, a kindred spirit who gets your pain." Even more broadly, she hopes that it "speaks to those who have not yet experienced the devastating effects of a loved one's dementia on family and friends."[39] As did Ellis, Richardson follows the chronology of her husband's decline, describing various stages in painstaking (and painful) detail. An index identifies this as a piece of nonfiction writing, as something "other" than a simple memoir. But Richardson's index, while locating items of information (Alzheimer's support group, Benadryl, memory care) makes no reference to any sociological writing, concepts, or theory. Much like Amy Bloom's recent memoir *In Love*, it takes us through the experience of being a caregiver to someone suffering from dementia, but unlike Mindy Fried's *Caring for Red* and Deborah Cohan's *Welcome to Wherever We Are*, Richardson does not locate that experience in any broader sociocultural context or use that experience to make any broader conceptual or theoretical point.[40] (In fact Bloom's memoir, by offering explicit information about the resources available to someone who might choose to die, provides more contextual information.) At the end, one might ask in what way (or even whether) Richardson's piece reflects the sociological training, insights, or perceptions of its author.[41]

In evocative autoethnography, the two forms of memoir and sociology can come close, if not merge. Both evocative autoethnographers and memoirists craft creative narratives, drawing from the writer's experience. Both use devices like description, setting, plot development, pacing, rhythm, character development, dialogue, and action to advance the story.[42] Both autoethnographers and memoirists "make themselves vulnerable in their writing." Both mine personal experiences for insights into "positionalities and relationships to inequalities."[43] Not surprisingly, then, critics claim that autoethnography offers nothing new or different from other forms of personal narrative, that it demonstrates, above all, an author's ego-driven quest to fulfill some personal ambition, and that it cannot be social science because it is neither driven by theory nor framed by analysis. And, not surprisingly, Ellis and Bochner reject these critiques, responding that the requirement of theory and analysis—whether wittingly or not—serves the interests of one class of academics over another, in this case story analysts over storytellers.[44]

Other Autoethnographic Approaches

By and large, the debates within autoethnography revolve around the question of how much analysis—if any—to include. But others claim that the conflicts within autoethnography are not limited to whether one is being either analytic or evocative. Robin Boylorn and Mark Orbe, in the introduction to *Critical Autoethnography: Intersecting Cultural Identities in Everyday Life*, argue that autoethnography must provide a "critical lens." Challenging the assumption that personal writing will always reproduce hegemonic norms and values, they insist that a critical lens can "open a space of resistance between the individual and the collective." And they continue, "In this space, the individual not only focuses on how lived experiences are affected by the dominant social order, but also seeks to defy and deconstruct this order."[45] The critical lens, as Tony Adams writes, can be informed by "feminist, critical race, queer, postcolonial, indigenous, and crip sensibilities—that focus intentionally, and fiercely, on identifying and remedying social harms and injustices."[46] Tasha Dunn, author of *Talking White Trash: Mediated Representations and Lived Experiences of White Working-Class People*, places herself within this tradition as she offers both her own account of her biography and that of other people similarly situated.[47]

Common Ground?

Given the contempt Ellis and Bochner hold for analysis and the doubts of Anderson and others as to whether the writings of Ellis and Bochner qualify as social science, it is hard to find common ground between these two extremes. Yet an entire range of "autoethnographical" works exist, some veering more in one direction, others in the other. Moreover, these works do have some common features.

Like other sociologists, autoethnographers can, and sometimes do, draw on a variety of sources including "participant observation, interviews, conversational engagement, focus groups, narrative analysis, artifact analysis, archival research, journaling, field notes, thematic analysis, description, context, interpretation, and storytelling."[48] But unlike "traditional ethnography," autoethnographers make the self highly visible, engage in strong "reflexivity," and make themselves vulnerable as they craft narratives "that attempt to evoke and capture the lived experiences of the researcher (and coparticipants, as applicable) in relation to the phenomena under study."[49]

This approach to social science can (and often does) have significant advantages for teaching sociology. The texts are accessible and reader-friendly. They can (and often do) provide vehicles for self-understanding, self-reflection, and self-examination for *both* the reader and the writer.

This understanding might, as Heewon Chang argues, lead to transformation, on the part of both the researcher and readers.[50] But these texts undoubtedly raise questions about their status as a unique form of sociology or even as a form of sociology at all. Does anything distinguish autoethnographic writing from, on the one hand, memoir (for evocative autoethnography) and, on the other hand, any sociological work (for analytic autoethnography) that involves reflexive participant observation? Who gets to define a given work as autoethnography? And what criteria should be applied to judging an autoethnographical work? These questions could usefully be discussed in a classroom.

In the next chapter, Middlebury College sociologist Rebecca Tiger (author of *Judging Addicts: Drug Courts and Coercion in the Justice System*, among other works) argues for classroom writing assignments that draw on personal experience as a mechanism for learning a discipline that may be new to students. In the tradition of Merton, she calls these assignments "sociological autobiography" and promotes them as a way for students to practice sociological analysis. She also discusses her own creative writing that draws on her firsthand experiences in the form of short memoirs to express herself outside of disciplinary constraints and, occasionally, as a way to return to sociology. But unlike the autoethnographers discussed above, she argues that this form of writing is not, in and of itself, a sociological method. Rather, she thinks of memoir as its own practice (and not "just" a technique for acquiring the skills of sociological analysis).

8

Writing to Learn

BY REBECCA TIGER

The previous chapter explored the arguments of those who suggest that writing about the self constitutes a method for doing sociology. In this chapter I discuss personal writing differently. I argue that an assignment asking students to write a short "sociological autobiography" is a useful tool for teaching sociology both to new and to more advanced undergraduates. Although what they produce is probably not "yet" sociology, I contend it is good practice for acquiring sociological insights. I also describe my own involvement in writing creative pieces drawn from my life experiences and discuss how that practice has enabled me to move beyond, and also back to, sociology as an academic discipline.

Teaching with Personal/Autobiographical Writing

Personal writing is a tool that can enhance the teaching of sociological concepts. While writing an autobiographical piece is not in and of itself *doing* sociology, when a sociological framework is applied to the writing, it can call on insights that are at the core of the sociological imagination. Thus, assignments that ask for memoir-style writing can be helpful in the classroom, perhaps especially in lower-level classes where students are just beginning to see themselves, and the world around them, through the lens of the sociological imagination (see box 8.1).[1]

Box 8.1: Rebecca Tiger's Assignment on Sociological Autobiography

In *600 words*, I want you to tell your sociological autobiography. The sociological imagination involves placing your specific biography in an historical context and linking your personal troubles to social issues. It is, in essence, understanding that you are an *individual* in a *society*.

The question, then, is how do we know we are part of this society? *Social facts* are the vehicle through which we are *integrated* into the beliefs of a society and *regulated* into adhering to them (often through approval/praise when we follow them or punishment when we violate them).

In these *600 words* you will take an aspect of your story and use it to reveal something about a social fact (or facts) that have governed your life. You could take one incident that reveals something about how you have been governed by a social fact or facts, using it as a way to illustrate the external and coercive nature of social facts. You could write about a time when you have either directly or indirectly enforced social facts on to others. Specific details help to illustrate the example you pick. You do not need to tell me your whole life story.

There are many iterations you can take in this short piece. The key is to show rather than tell! You don't need to reiterate to me Mills's definition of the "sociological imagination" or Durkheim's definition of "social facts." You will *show* me them in action through the story you write. And you will tell it in *600 words*!

When I teach introductory classes, I emphasize that sociology is a theoretical and data-oriented field. I also stress that it is not a set of opinions, assumptions, or statements about how the world is (or should be). At its most basic level, sociology starts with curiosity, with *questions*. And although as professional sociologists we ask questions in our own scholarly work and may require that advanced students also do so, I believe it is unrealistic to expect students new to the discipline to conduct a research project where they develop theoretically informed questions—and then design research protocols, collect and analyze data, and explain their findings. For this reason, it makes good sense to offer students a chance to think of themselves as the starting point—they are the first data to be examined, the first subject to ask questions about.

The building blocks of sociology, whether we call them social facts or something else, contain within them highly appropriate entry points for students. I find that people new to sociology often want to jump to explanations for what they see. Autobiographical assignments hold them back, making sure they take the first steps. These first steps are primarily about observation. How does gender or race or class or religion or sexuality or age or any other social category operate in our lives? What does it look like? What is its texture? To teach students how to begin to answer these questions, we can ask as a first assignment that they write a brief "sociological autobiography," describing a moment, an episode, or a scene where social facts operated in their life. This first step, then, is an occasion for them to understand the components of social facts, primarily their collective and coercive nature.[2]

Because description is a key component of this kind of carefully devised memoir-style writing assignment, the assignment embodies the principle "show don't tell." Students can easily list the categories that govern their lives, the constraints they face, and the ones they impose on others. A sociological autobiography asks that they illustrate these and bring them to life. An example: I had a student who wrote about the struggles they faced being an overweight child. Instead of telling the reader it was hard, this student portrayed difficulty by describing a particularly fraught scene: the school cafeteria. They detailed how they agonized over their food choices and eating in front of their peers. Minutiae such as clanging dishes, institutional fluorescent lighting, the fear of dropping the tray, stares from classmates who watched but avoided eating with them provided depth. But this student did something even more complex: they also talked about the validation they received at home from parents and grandparents who squeezed their chubby cheeks and expressed love through food. In this short piece, this student showed the conflicting way the social facts of weight and food both in the past and in the present operate in their lives.

My colleague Margaret Nelson used a personal writing assignment at the end of a second-level undergraduate course on the sociology of education. More specifically, she asked students to provide a sociological account of their educational careers, to explain how they ended up being students at an elite, private liberal arts college.[3] When she had been successful in her teaching, the best of her students were able to *show* in concrete detail that they understood how their own biography intersected with larger social and historical forces; to her great joy, they demonstrated that they had acquired a "sociological imagination."

Memoir-style assignments like these ask students to learn how to do what sociologists strive to be good at: observing without judgment. The "without judgment" piece is difficult for all of us, and perhaps especially for students. For this reason, we cannot simply assign personal writing and assume students will understand what it means to withhold assessment. While these assignments are not full-fledged memoir, I do want students to link their story to issues, to show their public connection. The injunction to write about oneself can lead to essays where students laud their individual choices while negatively judging those of others. This is possibly the greatest pitfall of these types of assignments.

Let me illustrate with an example from another student enrolled in the same introductory course. This student also addressed their struggle with their body and their weight when they were young. They wrote about how they came from a family they described as unhealthy and overweight, and they explained that the shame they felt about their parents and their sedentary "lifestyle" led them to start exercising and pursuing "healthy" ways of eating. They concluded that the social fact (and fear) of fatness was good because it pushed them to change, to become athletic and trim. When I commented critically on the essay, the student retorted, "This is my experience, so how can you question it?"

Rather than allowing the student to rest there, I worked with them to understand that this piece was making an evaluative argument, in this case that "shame is good." And I explained that they were not prepared to fully understand the argumentative nature of the piece precisely because they had not yet worked through the socially constructed nature of the categories they were using uncritically. In this instance, asking the student to address their feelings helped: I suggested the student could think about what it was like to have to be so vigilant and how the fear of fatness become such an ingrained part of their identity.

Techniques for Making Personal Writing Assignments Effective

One way to make memoir-style writing assignments effective is to tell students that they should not tie it all up with a tidy conclusion. Students who have been trained in high school to write with a thesis statement that makes an argument, three body paragraphs, and a final one that restates the introduction with new evidence inevitably want to write that summary paragraph. Therefore, it is important to show them that personal writing can take different forms: it can be impressionistic; it can be nonlinear. It is also inherently introspective.

At the same time, because these are not apt descriptions of sociology, writing assignments taking these forms and embodying the personal teach sociology only when they are accompanied by an understanding of the social. How did a student who controls their body through strict diet and exercise regimes come to understand this behavior as "good"? What are the social cues they receive that enforce certain social norms? Sociological memoirs must attend to these types of concerns. We are, after all, teaching sociological concepts and sociology is an outward facing discipline. Feelings matter essentially for how they are socially produced.

We can also tell students that there are right and wrong ways to answer the questions we might pose when we ask students to write a sociological autobiography. This might sound counterintuitive. How can a student's understanding of their individual experiences be assessed in this way? How can we grade these pieces as right or wrong?

First, we explain that we are treating these essays as *illustrations* of sociological concepts. We can make it clear that the examples they choose to write about, the details they include, and the connections they make are all there for the purpose of showing that as students they understand the sociology they have read and discussed. Just as not every fact is a social fact, not every recounting of experience illustrates sociological ideas. The choice of what to write about and the way they go about that writing are mechanisms by which students can show they are beginning to understand sociology.

A second thing we can do to make this kind of assignment effective is to set word limits. Tell students that these are not diary entries, free-writes, or response papers. They are stories and illustrations, and to function as an entrée to sociology, students must use language that is clear and considered. Limits help because they require students to ponder every word they use. Does this word accurately convey what they want it to? The guidelines of "flash" writing suggest a first assignment of six hundred words; this is useful in the sociology classroom setting as well.[4] Not surprisingly, some students balk at this, while others think that it will be easy (especially when they are also writing a fifteen-page paper for another class at the same time!). But, as most of us know, it can be hard to communicate complex ideas with few words. And as most of us also know, it is difficult to get students to revise, edit, and proofread. Memoir-style assignments require all these strategies to be effective. Thus, I also explore the issues of writing and revising in my courses and have moved to setting aside an entire class session to talk about effective writing. I also give them several prompt-based writing exercises to help them develop the ideas they will subsequently elaborate on in their sociological autobiography.

Finally, to return to a point that is worth repeating, I do not think that this kind of personal writing is sociology even though it can have sociological elements such as placing personal experience in a social and historical context. Rather, I believe these assignments allow students to practice sociology through the illustration of sociological concepts. Personal writing is thus a useful tool for getting students to connect to sociology through an examination of their lives. It may be especially beneficial in lower-level classes where a concept as basic as "institutions" might be too big for them to grasp, although they can recognize that they have already interacted with schools, families, medicine, and social media. Similar assignments might also be useful as a way to explore issues in more advanced courses. In fact, the literature on teaching sociology includes a range of different courses in which personal writing assignments have been used, including medical sociology, the sociology of religion, the sociology of the body, and the sociology of education.[5]

Whether used in entry courses or with more advanced students, these assignments offer a foundation for students to learn how to look outward as they look inward, to apply the categories and concepts they are acquiring, to then attain the ability to ask theoretically informed questions, and to analyze the data they collect from the world around them.

Can These Assignments Circumvent AI Technology?

Out of curiosity, I asked ChatGPT to try to complete the assignment of writing a sociological autobiography. First, I asked in a general way, "Write an essay for an introductory sociology course in the form of a sociological autobiography. Limit it to 600 words." The response was clunky: "As I embark on this sociological journey, I find myself introspecting, reflecting, and unraveling the intricate web of experiences that have shaped my understanding of the world around me. This sociological autobiography delves into the various dimensions of my life that have contributed to the formation of my social identity, shedding light on the interplay between personal encounters and societal forces."

I then asked again, using some of the precise language of the assignment I give my students. This time, ChatGPT told me that "as an AI language model," it lacks "personal experiences and biographical data." It then continued with what it could do for me: "I can simulate a sociological autobiography by crafting a narrative that encapsulates the essence of the sociological imagination and the integration of personal biography within broader societal contexts." And it did just that, with an essay that also did precisely the reverse of what I ask of my students. It *told* rather than *showed*. That is, it applied sociological concepts to an imagined life, but it did not explore *how* that imagined life was intimately tied to personal insights or sociological understanding. For example, in the paragraph below, the "author" tells us that it "encountered the power dynamics of gender roles" but does not explain just how those dynamics work or why it then became, in its words, a "feminist."

> Education became my gateway to understanding the complexities of society. As I progressed through school, my interactions with peers from various backgrounds exposed me to a myriad of perspectives. It was during my high school years that I encountered the power dynamics of gender roles. The expectations imposed on me as a female student ignited a desire to explore the wider implications of such expectations in society. This personal trouble led me to delve into the feminist movement, where I learned to dissect the patriarchal structures that perpetuated gender inequalities. I realized that my individual struggles were emblematic of a broader societal construct.

I could work with the student who handed in an essay like this, but I would not accept it for the assignment, and I would require a rewrite.

The Evidence of Effectiveness

Some academics have assessed the effectiveness of personal writing assignments through questionnaires distributed to students at the end of a course. Sociologist Peta Cook, for example, found that personal writing assignments actually "actively engaged the students and enhanced their sociological learning by stimulating their critical thinking on the relationship between their lived experiences and the social."[6] Similarly, sociology professor Alem Kebede discerned that although students found the assignments challenging, they stretched themselves and believed that they had a deeper understanding of themselves and others.[7] Recently, sociologists Susan Mannon and Eileen Camfield reviewed a number of such instances of the use of these assignments.[8] Taken as a whole the studies showed that this kind of assignment enhanced interest in a course, helped students consider social-structural forces at work rather than focusing on individualistic or psychological explanations, and gave students an opportunity to write in the first person.

But for all these positive effects, as suggested above, problems exist in the use of these assignments. Evaluation raises several complex issues. Aside from the fact that there is no way of knowing whether students accurately and honestly report their experiences, teachers end up grading them on those reports. Students might come to feel that they are assessed on issues irrelevant to classroom learning: Are their lives interesting enough? Are they open enough? Moreover, given the power differential between teachers and their students, we might ask whether it is ethical to require students to reveal personal (and sometimes even traumatic) parts of their pasts.[9]

In response to these concerns, we might remind students that although the essays they write are subjective, they are assigned to assess sociological learning. We might also remind students that we are not interested in learning about their lives but that we are interested in learning how they understand themselves and, even more so, in learning how they understand sociology. Moreover, we might indicate that these types of writing assignments share the same problems of any assignment that veers from an objective test of a limited set of ideas.

Writing Creative Nonfiction as a Sociologist

Just as personal writing can be an entry point to sociology, it can also be a tool for creatively exploring ideas one has grappled with for years and thus a way to further illuminate sociology. I have written academic pieces about prison, drug policy, the law and courts, the history of addiction, and more recently media and celebrity. I observe the world through institutional structures, which is a classically meso-level approach to sociology. Surprisingly, the freedom to write creatively without the requirement to theorize has allowed me to make new sociological connections that were not as easy to make when I was adhering to an academic style. Thus, writing memoir-like pieces about important episodes has had an epistemological function as much as a creative one. Let me give an example from my own life.

During the past year I have spent several hours a week in a "memory care" facility with my mother who is dying of cancer and has dementia.[10] I talk with other residents, keep my mother company in the common area, eat meals in the dining room, interact with health aides and nursing staff, and participate in the caregiving of other residents when I see they need a push of their wheelchair or help remembering where they are or which room is theirs. I have even stopped residents who wandered off toward the highway, torn (I confess) between wanting them to be free while understanding that their memory impairments will not serve them well outside the facility where they might easily get lost or hit by a car.

My first instinct when my mother moved to this facility was to understand it through the lens of Erving Goffman's "total institutions."[11] I teach his essays on this topic every year in my "Deviance & Social Control" class. I cannot help but reflect through his insights while sitting in an institution that strips people of one identity to build up another, as residents talk about going back to homes their adult children have sold and to lives that are no more.

But Goffman's approach was of little use when I thought about putting down on paper what I was seeing and what I was experiencing. Was it sufficient to depict the subtle interactions, repetitions, joys, suffering, caring, and indignities that happen in this particular institution? I felt not, and instead I turned to the genre of memoir/creative nonfiction, an approach that allowed me the freedom to convey these observations and events without the constraints of the discipline (in two senses) of sociology. I could now describe my heartbreak with my mother's dementia and my anguish watching the sweet and painful ways residents in this facility care for each other even though they often forget who the other person is the next morning. In other words, total institutions had become immediate and very personal. I had to write differently.

At the same time, this new, more intimate approach, an approach that allows for stylistic and narrative freedom, has strengthened my sociological insights. For example, I wrote a braided story that impressionistically links memory care centers, prisons, schools, and families. In the process, I was able to further grasp the similarities between and among these specific sites of social control and identity construction.

However, I view my creative writing, even when it leads to new sociological insights, as a practice but not a sociological method, and I do not label it "autoethnography." Yes, I draw on sociological insights. That is, my writing inevitably reflects that I am someone attuned to institutions, trained to connect the personal and the social, the biographical and the historical; of course my writing is influenced by my academic background. But this other way of writing, whether I call it memoir or something else, is a way of conveying what I cannot within the discipline of sociology because of its conventions. To be clear, I am not saying that I consider these conventions a limit to or defect of sociology. And I would not argue for opening sociology up to include memoir and creative nonfiction as sociological *method*. Nor would I want someone to read my flash pieces about my mother's facility and think they are offering some analytic framework for understanding dementia, aging, family, institutions of confinement, class, race, religion, or labor, although all these factors appear in my stories.[12] As Nelson argues in chapter 5, I too think pieces like these could be *used* in a classroom as supplemental material, as a way to think about broad issues like contemporary aging. But I do not believe they are sociology per se.

Just as personal writing assignments can be a useful way of teaching sociology, memoir-style writing can be an effective tool for more advanced sociologists, a way for them to look at their research specialties with a new lens. But I do not view what I ask of students and what I do on my own as equivalent. I want students to create one scene where social facts are clearly highlighted so they can start connecting their personal selves to social structure; I want them to practice working with sociological concepts. Memoir through the craft form called "the braided essay" makes nonlinear connections between seemingly disparate topics.[13] It can move back and forth in time and pick up on new themes as it expands. When successful, this movement back and forth in historical, institutional, and social location fosters breadth and depth through its juxtapositions and thus allows for analytic as well as creative connections. This approach requires a more advanced grasp of sociology (than is available to introductory students) as well as of memoir with its distinct form and craft elements, both of which differ from academic sociology. For these reasons, I think of it as a practice that incorporates sociology, not as practicing—or even doing—sociology.

In short, personal writing can be a beneficial practice for all sociologists. This kind of writing can help students learn basic sociological concepts by applying them to their own life. Writing memoir also offers advanced sociologists the chance to connect across sociological subfields, allowing us to see the connections among social phenomena beyond the confines of substantive specialty and disciplinary writing conventions.

Conclusion

In response to Peter Stein's memoir, *A Boy's Journey: From Nazi-Occupied Prague to Freedom in America*, and his related essay, "Biography, Trauma, the Holocaust and the Sociological Eye," Williams College sociologist Christina Simko suggests that "no genre is better equipped to draw together the literary and the sociological than memoir."[1] While memoir might well be more "creative" than the bulk of what passes for sociology today, its authors promise to adhere to a standard of truthfulness, even as they acknowledge interpretation shaped by "the natural distortions of memory and perspective." Moreover, Simko argues that good literature (in the form of memoir) and good sociology have similarities. First, both "capture the role and weight of *contingency* in human life." Second, both offer "audiences a window onto worlds they cannot experience firsthand." Third, both have the capacity to cultivate "'humane sympathy,' especially by probing what Alison Pugh calls 'meta-feelings' or 'how we feel about how we feel'"; thus they have the "power of culture to penetrate our inner landscapes."[2] Finally, Simko writes, through "encounters with difference," memoir and sociology both can fuel the imagination.[3]

Not only do the two forms have similarities, but first-person narratives have had a significant place in the development of sociological thought. Beginning with W. I. Thomas and Florian Znaniecki's 1927 *The Polish Peasant in Europe and America*, sociologists have drawn on a variety of such writing as a methodological approach, a way to place individual experiences, attitudes, and values at the center of an analysis. Since that time, many sociologists including Robert K. Merton (with his interest in sociological autobiography), Barbara Laslett and Barrie

Thorne (with their interest in life histories), and Mary Jo Maynes, Jennifer Pierce, and Barbara Laslett (with their interest in personal narrative) have adopted some variation of this approach.[4]

The chapters in this book have built on, and expanded, this perspective. In the first chapter I linked the memoir boom to what has been called the "narrative turn" in sociology, a turn that helped bring personal writing to the fore. In the next chapter I introduced ideas about our understanding of the authors behind memoirs, the constraints on the stories they could tell, and the audience's expectations of truthfulness.

In chapter 3, the first in part II, I reviewed various autobiographical writings by sociologists (including those collected by Laslett and Thorne) both for the issues they discussed as well as for a broader analysis of how they informed our understanding of the theoretical and practical (i.e., career) concerns of different groups of sociologists at different moments in time. The fact that a wide variety of collections of personal essays exists demonstrates well the significance sociologists have placed in drawing on autobiographical writing to illuminate developments in the field, explain theoretical debates, and provide access to understanding the social processes surrounding the creation and transmission of knowledge. Because so few of the personal writings of sociologists examined an early research experience itself (as a way in which knowledge is created, transmitted, and changed), in chapter 4 I focused on three prominent sociologists for what they could tell us about how scholars might explain their methodology and respond to changing criteria of evaluation.

Most of the collections of essays discussed in chapter 3 let the memoir writers speak for themselves. The introductory essays and conclusions provide some generalizations about content (e.g., about careers as sociologists) but do not subsume the individual voices. Of course, sociologists are not the only groups of individuals whose life histories are anthologized: scholars have also collected essays from academics who grew up as members of the working class, gay men and lesbians, adoptees and women who have relinquished babies for adoption, among many others. But few social scientists have gone beyond collecting essays from similarly situated individuals to show how memoirs themselves could provide data for the sociological analysis of issues. In chapter 6 I reviewed four studies that do just that. In those four studies the memoirs become the evidence from which sociologists draw generalizations about a specific topic. This chapter, in turn, built on the preceding one in which I reflected on how memoirs excite the sociological imagination. In both chapters I considered questions to be asked when using memoirs as fodder for sociological analysis. And in both chapters I approached memoirs as stories we might think about, rather than as stories we might think with.[5]

In chapter 7 I presented the view of those who would argue that this is the wrong way altogether to approach memoir and even the wrong way altogether to read and write sociology. In what has been called "evocative autoethnography" the difference between the two forms of memoir and sociology becomes difficult to discern. While sociologists writing evocative autoethnography often do so from the perspective of individuals trained to perceive sociocultural influences on human action, that training might not be obvious in pieces that intentionally downplay analysis. And many memoirists, even without academic training, draw on their own insights into issues like race, class, and gender to inform their writing. Indeed, as analytic autoethnographer Robert Courtney Smith suggests, authors of the two forms—memoir and evocative autoethnography—can use similar devices, including making themselves "vulnerable in their writing" and examining "personal epiphanies for insight into their positionalities and relationships to inequalities."[6] In the final chapter, Rebecca Tiger considered how the use of autobiographical storytelling enables individuals to write themselves into sociological knowledge and why sociological autobiography might be useful for classroom assignments.

Ultimately, however useful memoir might be for sociology, and however similar they might be in what they can do for and to us, the two are not the same. Memoirs remain in the domain of a single subjectivity, exploring specific events, periods, or themes from the perspective of an individual author's life. Not all memoir writers have the same purposes in mind when they choose to narrate their lives: they might want to share personal insights, to get revenge, to arouse concern about a specific social issue, to engage in self-aggrandizement, to remember, or to interrogate their own experience. But those purposes will be different from the purpose of sociology, which is to draw on empirical evidence to provide (testable) explanations for, and theories of, social phenomena. Good memoirs can become data for analysis, excite the imagination, provide examples of significant social processes; writing our own can enable us to better understand sociological concepts and theory. But useful as they may be *for* sociologists, and similar as they may be in their capacities, they are not good sociology. And we need both—good sociology and good memoirs—to help us better understand ourselves and our relationships with the worlds in which we live.

NOTES

PREFACE

1 Nelson, *Keeping Family Secrets*.
2 Bjorklund, *Interpreting the Self*, ix.
3 Abel and Nelson, *Limited Choices*.
4 Abel and Nelson, *Farm & Wilderness Summer Camps*.

INTRODUCTION

1 Frank, *Wounded Storyteller*; Frank, *Letting Stories Breathe*; Irvine, Pierce, and Zussman, *Narrative Sociology*; Maynes, Pierce, and Laslett, *Telling Stories*.
2 Carey, "Parents and Professionals"; Kuchler, *Images of Memory*; Maynes, Pierce, and Laslett, *Telling Stories*.
3 Genzlinger, "Problem with Memoirs."
4 Abel, *Living in Death's Shadow*, 8.
5 Frank, *Wounded Storyteller*, 21.
6 Perry, *Friends, Lovers, and the Big Terrible Thing*; McCurdy, *I'm Glad My Mom Died*.
7 Caldwell, *Let's Take the Long Way Home*.
8 Olsen, *If You Tell*; Robb, *Don't Think, Dear*; Hendrickson, *Life on Delay*. For a discussion of memoirs from the wealthy, see Young, "It's My Privilege."
9 Hampl and May, "Introduction," Kindle loc. 65.
10 Vance, *Hillbilly Elegy*.
11 Coates, *Between the World and Me*. For a good discussion of this difference, see Mack and Alexander, "Ethics of Memoir."
12 Malcolm X, *Autobiography of Malcolm X*; Moody, *Coming of Age in Mississippi*.
13 Even longer lists of terms are offered by Smith and Watson in *Reading Autobiography*.
14 Couser, *Memoir*; Rak, *Boom!*
15 See, for example, the ways in which personal narratives—including memoirs—have been analyzed by social scientists including Frank, *Wounded Storyteller*; Frank, "Illness and Autobiographical Work"; Irvine, Pierce, and Zussman,

Narrative Sociology; Maynes, Pierce, and Laslett, *Telling Stories*; Frank, *Letting Stories Breathe*.

16 Du Bois, *Autobiography*.

17 Maynes, Pierce, and Laslett, *Telling Stories*, 77.

18 Maynes, Pierce, and Laslett.

19 Smith and Watson, *Reading Autobiography*, 274.

20 Allison, *Bastard Out of Carolina*; Greenhalgh, *Under the Medical Gaze*; Toews, *Swing Low*.

21 Couser, *Memoir*; Adams, "Almost Famous."

22 I am thankful to Robert Zussman for this insight even as it gets muddled.

23 Albom, *Tuesdays with Morrie*.

24 Beverley, "Testimonio, Subalternity, and Narrative Authority," 571.

25 Latina Feminist Group, *Telling to Live*.

26 Perez and Cantú, "Talking Testimonio," 151.

27 Perez and Cantú; Menchú, *I, Rigoberta Menchú*.

28 Perez and Cantú, "Talking Testimonio."

29 Reyes and Rodríguez, "Testimonio."

30 See Moehringer, "Notes from Prince Harry's Ghostwriter."

31 Maynes, Pierce, and Laslett, *Telling Stories*, 77.

32 Rak, *Boom!*

33 Obama, *Becoming*.

34 Laslett and Thorne, "Life Histories of a Movement," 4.

35 Mendelsohn, *Odyssey*.

36 Bessire, *Running Out*.

37 Gordon-Reed, *On Juneteenth*.

38 Chávez, *Taco Testimony*. For a discussion of this book, see Revels, "Talking Tacos."

39 I also emphasize those memoirs in which the authors themselves write their stories rather than relying on ghostwriters.

40 For excellent examples of that form, see Bechdel, *Fun Home*; Chast, *Can't We Talk about Something More Pleasant?*; Kimball, *And Now I Spill the Family Secrets*.

41 Bjorklund, *Interpreting the Self*, 168.

42 Rothman, "Writing Ourselves in Sociology"; Rothman, *Weaving a Family*.

43 Davidman, *Motherloss*.

44 Daniels, *Nice White Ladies*.

45 Miller, *But Enough about Me*; Rak, *Boom!*

46 Larson, *Memoir and the Memoirist*.

47 Although the goals of each of the chapters are distinctive, I acknowledge considerable overlap among them in theoretical and methodological issues *and* in appropriate examples. I draw on different examples for each chapter from among the astonishingly large corpus of memoirs.

1. THE MEMOIR BOOM AND THE NARRATIVE TURN

1 Yagoda, *Memoir*.
2 Yagoda, loc. 3313.
3 Yagoda, loc. 120.
4 Yagoda, loc. 426.
5 Rak, *Boom!*, 116.
6 Couser, *Memoir*, 3.
7 Adams, "Almost Famous," 45.
8 Genzlinger, "Problem with Memoirs."
9 Miller, "But Enough about Me."
10 Yagoda, *Memoir*, loc. 3312.
11 Smith, "What Memoir Forgets."
12 See Rak, *Boom!*, loc. 1674, citing Miller, "But Enough about Me." See also historian Patrick Smith, who believes the memoir boom to be the outcome of a distinctly *American* failing, not because people in the United States are particularly lacking in the "self" or publish in a capitalist society but because since the Cold War we as a nation have been unable to "come to terms with what we have done—at home and abroad, to ourselves and others." Unable to acknowledge our wrongs, Smith argues, we turn our history into fiction. Smith, "What Memoir Forgets."
13 Larson, *Memoir and the Memoirist*, 188.
14 Karr, *Liars' Club*; Karr, *Art of Memoir*; Garner, "Mary Karr."
15 Gopnik, "Annie Ernaux's Justly Deserved Nobel."
16 Johnson, *Geography of the Heart*; Hampl and May, "Introduction."
17 Johnson, "Lion and the Lamb," loc. 260.
18 Couser, *Memoir*, 26.
19 For examples of books written by people with autism, see Higashida, *Reason I Jump*; Williams, *Nobody Nowhere*; Nazeer, *Send in the Idiots*. See also the list from the Boston Public Library, "Life on the Spectrum: Biographies of People with Autism Spectrum Disorder" (2024), https://bpl.bibliocommons.com. For examples of books written by people with Down syndrome, see Egan and Egan, *More Alike Than Different*, and Kingsley and Levitz, *Count Us In*. And for books written by someone with Alzheimer's, see Mitchell, *Somebody I Used to Know*.
20 May, "Confessions of a Memoir Thief," loc. 1202. For a similar point for historians, see Buss, *Repossessing the World*.
21 Becker, "We in the Me."
22 Johnson, "Lion and the Lamb."
23 Rak, *Boom!*
24 Rak, loc. 717.
25 Conway, *Road from Coorain*.
26 Conway, *When Memory Speaks*, 7.
27 Larson, *Memoir and the Memoirist*.
28 Gates, *Colored People*.

29 Maynes, Pierce, and Laslett, *Telling Stories.*
30 Ewick and Silbey, "Subversive Stories and Hegemonic Tales."
31 Irvine, Pierce, and Zussman, *Narrative Sociology*, 3. Several essays in the volume edited by Irvine, Pierce, and Zussman help define narrative: see, for example, Polkinghorne, "Explanatory Narrative Research"; Bruner, "Life as Narrative."
32 Many have noted that the narrative turn did not represent the first time "life history" has been an important approach in sociology. Most notably, they point to the Chicago School and the frequent use of interview as a way of probing the surface (Atkinson, "Narrative Turn or Blind Alley?"). Francesca Polletta argues that before the "narrative turn" sociology approached narrative in two ways: symbolic interactionists interested in what they called "accounts" fashioned to avert threats to self-interest and status, and ethnomethodological studies of how "people used stories in conversation to maintain interactional order." But after 1980, stories were no longer things people told but "things that people lived," the way (as individuals and/or collectivities) they fashioned identity from the materials available in their society and the way that they made sense of their lives. Polletta, "'It Was like a Fever.'" See also Polletta et al., "Sociology of Storytelling."
33 Vaughan, *Challenger Launch Decision*; Duneier, *Sidewalk*; Goffman, *On the Run.*
34 Irvine, Pierce, and Zussman, *Narrative Sociology*, 4.
35 Frank, *Wounded Storyteller.*
36 Maynes, Pierce, and Laslett, *Telling Stories*, loc. 90.
37 Maynes, Pierce, and Laslett, loc. 93; Laslett and Thorne, *Feminist Sociology*, 2.
38 In her review of Laslett and Thorne, Judith Gerson makes these points: "Laslett and Thorne understand personal narratives as an alternative way to theorize and as a means to 'illuminate relationships between social structure and human agency, between social circumstances and the changing construction of knowledge' (19). Feminist sociology is a case study, one which illustrates how 'power, resources for organization, identity, and feelings about them are key dimensions of the intellectual and social processes from which new forms of scholarship emerge.'" Gerson, "Review of *Feminist Sociology*," 912.
39 Goetting, "Introduction," 9.
40 Goetting, 10–13.
41 Crenshaw, "Mapping the Margins."
42 Collins, *Black Feminist Thought.*
43 See, for example, Preston, *Member of the Family*; Merla, *Boys Like Us*; Beam, "Brother to Brother"; Smith, *Black Men / White Men.*
44 Laslett and Thorne, "Life Histories of a Movement," 3.
45 Whitlock, *Soft Weapons*, 9.
46 See, for example, Whitlock, *Soft Weapons*; Ewick and Silbey, "Subversive Stories and Hegemonic Tales."

2. SELF, STORY, AND VERACITY

1 DeGloma, *Seeing the Light*; Snyder, "Review of *Seeing the Light*," 126.
2 Couser, *Memoir*, 174.
3 Smith and Watson, *Reading Autobiography*, 70.
4 Kaplan, "Lady of the Lake," loc. 1377.
5 Bjorklund, *Interpreting the Self*; Frank, *Wounded Storyteller*.
6 Eakin, *How Our Lives Become Stories*, ix.
7 Eakin, 47.
8 Eakin also acknowledges that in posing these as binaries we are likely to overlook the ways in which male autobiography can be relational and women's autobiography can be individualistic and narrative in character. On women's autobiography, see Jelinek, "Teaching Women's Autobiographies."
9 Kaplan, "Lady of the Lake," loc. 3283.
10 Bruner, "Self-Making and World-Making"; Bruner, "Narrative Creation of Self"; Bruner, "Life as Narrative."
11 Zussman, "Autobiographical Occasions"; Zussman, "Picturing the Self."
12 Laslett and Thorne, "Life Histories of a Movement."
13 Ewick and Silbey, "Subversive Stories and Hegemonic Tales."
14 Maynes, Pierce, and Laslett, *Telling Stories*.
15 Maynes, Pierce, and Laslett, 78.
16 Couser, *Memoir*; Smith and Watson, *Reading Autobiography*; Zussman, "Boy's Journey and the Journey to Freedom."
17 Couser, *Memoir*, 28.
18 Harrison and Smiley, *Kiss*.
19 Hodes, *My Hijacking*, 6.
20 Rak, *Boom!*, 50.
21 Williams et al., "15 Memoirs and Biographies to Read This Fall."
22 The memoirs included Zamora, *Solito*; Enninful, *Visible Man*; Beaton, *Ducks*; Hsu, *Stay True*; Manning, *README.txt*; Hill, *Uphill*; Samatar, *White Mosque*; Sehee, *I Want to Die but I Want to Eat Tteokbokki*; Newman and Newman, *Extraordinary Life of an Ordinary Man*; Perry, *Friends, Lovers, and the Big Terrible Thing*; Wenner, *Like a Rolling Stone*; Rickman, *Madly, Deeply*. The biographies included Worsley, *Agatha Christie*; Baldwin, *Martha Graham*; Boynton, *Wild*.
23 Hodes, *My Hijacking*.
24 Myers, *Thinning Blood*.
25 Grealy, *Autobiography of a Face*.
26 Couser, *Memoir*, 37.
27 Goetting, "Introduction," 15, emphasis added.
28 For a discussion that argues that social scientists make the same kinds of decisions about presentation, see Richardson, "Trash on the Corner." See also the discussion in chapter 7 on autoethnography.
29 Couser, *Memoir*, 80.

30 Couser.

31 Lejeune, "From Autobiography to Life-Writing."

32 Johnson, "Lion and the Lamb," loc. 229.

33 Johnson, loc. 292.

34 Frey, *Million Little Pieces.*

35 Rak, "Memoir, Truthiness, and the Power of Oprah."

36 These kinds of doubts were well expressed in Stephen Colbert's satirizing discourse of "truthiness" where gut feelings became more important than fact: Truthiness is "what I say is right, and [nothing] anyone else says could possibly be true." It's not only that I *feel* it to be true, but that *I* feel it to be true. There's not only an emotional quality, but there's a selfish quality. Rabin, "Stephen Colbert."

37 Mendelsohn, "But Enough about Me," 68.

38 Mortenson and Relin, *Three Cups of Tea.*

39 Krakauer, *Three Cups of Deceit.*

40 Stoll, *Rigoberta Menchú and the Story of All Poor Guatemalans.*

41 Grandin, *Who Is Rigoberta Menchú?*

42 Menchú, *I, Rigoberta Menchú*, 1.

43 Kavanagh and Rich, *Truth Decay*, 51.

44 Kakutani, *Death of Truth*, 69.

45 Kakutani has even harsher words for what he calls "moi criticism," or the practice on the part of academics of acknowledging how their own backgrounds might shape their analysis.

46 Mack and Alexander, "Ethics of Memoir."

47 Valentine, *When I Was White*, vii.

48 Kupfer, *Before and After Zachariah*, 2.

49 Davis, "Rich Cases."

50 Social scientists who anonymize their subjects do not have precisely the same problem. But they too use pseudonyms and change details of a person's life to protect that anonymity, which systematically—and necessarily—alters the facts.

51 Ribbens, "Facts or Fictions?," 87.

3. BECOMING AND BEING

1 Merton, "Some Thoughts on the Concept of Sociological Autobiography," 19.

2 Merton.

3 Zussman, "Autobiographical Occasions."

4 Page, *Fifty Years in the Sociological Enterprise*; Homans, *Coming to My Senses*; Bendix, *From Berlin to Berkeley*; Martindale, *Romance of a Profession*; Whyte, *Participant Observer*; Feyerabend, *Killing Time.*

5 Whyte, *Participant Observer*; Fox, *In the Field*; Berger, *Adventures of an Accidental Sociologist*; Turner, *Mad Hazard*; Etzioni, *My Brother's Keeper*; Henderson and Levy, *Race and the University.*

6   Du Bois, *Darkwater*; Du Bois, *Autobiography*; Du Bois, *Dusk of Dawn*.

7   Corona, *Night Class*; Gaines, *Misfit's Manifesto*. For a discussion of Gaines's book and its use in a classroom, see Ahlkvist, "Review of *A Misfit's Manifesto*."

8   Cottom, *Thick*; Reyes, *Academic Outsider*.

9   Lipset, "Steady Work"; Babbie, "Accidental Career."

10 Rossi, *Seasons of a Woman's Life*.

11 Zhou, *Accidental Sociologist in Asian American Studies*. See also Rios, *Punished*; Hansen, *Encounter on the Great Plains*.

12 Lazarsfeld, "Episode in the History of Social Research"; Riesman, "On Discovering and Teaching Sociology." In addition, crossing the line between biography and memoir, some have written essays in honor of someone else to show the influence of the other scholar's thought, career, and personal development on the field or on the writer's own life. These include (undoubt-edly among others) essays by Colfer on Peter McHugh (Colfer, "Peter McHugh"), Goertzel on Al Szymanski (Goertzel, "Albert Szymanski"), and Zubrzycki on Edward Shils (Zubrzycki, "Edward Shils").

13 Riley, *Sociological Lives*; Berger, *Authors of Their Own Lives*; Darling, "Introduction."

14 Orlans and Wallace, *Gender and the Academic Experience*; Goetting and Fenstermaker, *Individual Voices, Collective Visions*; Laslett and Thorne, *Feminist Sociology*.

15 Stanfield, *History of Race Relations Research*; Hunter, *New Black Sociologists*; Andersen and Zinn, *Moving from the Margins*.

16 Valverde and Dariotis, *Fight the Tower*; Buenavista, Jain, and Ledesma, *First-Generation Faculty of Color*; Hairston, *Ivory Tower*; Aikau, Erickson, and Pierce, *Feminist Waves, Feminist Generations*; Harris, "Foreword"; Gutiérrez y Muhs et al., *Presumed Incompetent*.

17 Stein, "Conclusion."

18 Berger, *Adventures of an Accidental Sociologist*.

19 Hess, "Accidental Sociologist," 40.

20 Zhou, *Accidental Sociologist in Asian American Studies*, x.

21 Babbie, "Accidental Career"; Babbie, *Practice of Social Research*.

22 Wrong, "Imagining the Real," 9.,

23 Willie, "Commentary on Sociological Lives," 165.

24 Andersen and Zinn, "Moving from the Margins," 11.

25 Bernard, "Woman's Twentieth Century," 324.

26 See the discussion of this in Goetting and Fenstermaker, *Individual Voices, Collective Visions*.

27 Pincus, "Sociological Memoir"; Hall, "Sociological Consequences of Choosing Radical Parents."

28 Simon, "Spreading the Sociological Imagination," 181.

29 Wingfield, "School Daze," 102.

30 Corona, *Night Class*, 22.

31 Gaines, *Misfit's Manifesto*, 156–57.

32 Gaines, 219.

33 Olick, "'Collective Memory,'" 27.

34 Coser, "Notes on a Double Career," 68; Coser, *Functions of Social Conflict*.

35 Gaines, *Misfit's Manifesto*, 225.

36 Smith, "Berkeley Education"; Smith, *Everyday World as Problematic*, 54–55.

37 Bernard, "Woman's Twentieth Century," 338.

38 Acker, "My Life as a Feminist Sociologist," 35.

39 Higginbotham, "Networking across Stages of a Career," 187.

40 Johnson, "For, By and About," 149.

41 Andersen and Zinn, "Moving from the Margins," 6.

42 Omi, "Thinking through Race," 54.

43 Hondagneu-Sotelo, "Shifting Boundaries," 137.

44 Wingfield, "School Daze," 103.

45 Glenn, "Looking Back in Anger?," 93.

46 Reyes, *Academic Outsider*, 1. See also Stacey, "Disloyal to the Disciplines"; Pierce, "Traveling from Feminism to Mainstream Sociology and Back"; and Zhou, *Accidental Sociologist in Asian American Studies*.

47 Berger, *Adventures of an Accidental Sociologist*, loc. 255.

48 Babbie, "Accidental Career"; Fox, *In the Field*.

49 Bendix, *From Berlin to Berkeley*, 213, 226.

50 Whyte, *Participant Observer*, 110.

51 DeVault, "Second Generation Story."

52 Garey and Hansen, *At the Heart of Work and Family*.

53 Pierce, "Traveling from Feminism to Mainstream Sociology and Back."

54 Moore, "'I Thought She Was One of Us!'"

55 Branch, "Life Histories on Transforming the Study of Racism"; Andersen, "From Clueless to Critical," 46.

56 Romero, "Critical Race Feminist," 95.

57 Segura, "I Change Myself," 78.

58 Andersen and Zinn, "Moving from the Margins," 7.

59 Dill, "From the Sandbox"; Segura, "I Change Myself," 84.

60 Pierce, "Traveling from Feminism to Mainstream Sociology and Back."

61 Lipset, "Steady Work," 17.

62 The exceptions to this generalization are a few sociologists whose wives also had academic careers—see, for example, Fred Pincus, who is married to Natalie Sokoloff, in Pincus, "Sociological Memoir."

63 On these issues, see Mason, Wolfinger, and Goulden, *Do Babies Matter?*

64 Daniels, "When We Were All Boys Together," 33.

65 Daniels, 36.

66 Smith, "Berkeley Education," 49.

67 Hochschild, "Inside the Clockwork of Male Careers," 126.

68 Stanfield, *History of Race Relations Research*.

69 Gutiérrez y Muhs et al., *Presumed Incompetent*; Harris, "Foreword."

70 For the most part, these early collections also did not address either sexuality or disability.

71 Lerum, "What's Love Got to Do with It?," 268.

72 Robinson, "Non-binary Embodiment," 425.

4. THE RESEARCH

1 Du Bois, *Darkwater*; Du Bois, *Autobiography*; Du Bois, *Dusk of Dawn*.

2 *TPN* is not Du Bois's dissertation: he received his PhD from Harvard with a dissertation on the history of the slave trade ("The Suppression of the African Slave-Trade," 1896). Nor was *TPN* his first piece of independent sociological research. While teaching at Wilberforce University, he conducted a study, published as "The Negroes of Farmville Virginia" (in *W. E. B. Du Bois on Sociology and the Black Community*); he does not discuss this study in any of his autobiographies, and it is not well known.

3 Whyte, *Street Corner Society*. Subsequently, Whyte began his sociological studies at the University of Chicago, where he submitted the printed manuscript, along with two published articles in which he included reviews of the literature, as his dissertation.

4 Fox, *In the Field*.

5 Fox, *Experiment Perilous*.

6 Du Bois, *Autobiography*, 195.

7 Du Bois, 195.

8 Du Bois, *Dusk of Dawn*, 30.

9 Du Bois, *Autobiography*, 187.

10 Du Bois, 198.

11 Du Bois, 199–200.

12 Several initial reviews praised this work highly (although it received no review in the *American Journal of Sociology*). In the *Annals*, Booth wrote, "Du Bois' study is exceptional and scholarly, and seems to realize his ideal of seeking the truth in the 'heart quality of fairness'" ("Review of *The Philadelphia Negro*," 100). In another review, this one in the *Journal of Political Economy*, Katharine Davis concluded, "The book, as a whole, is probably one of the most important contributions we have yet had toward the study of the negro problem in the United States" ("Condition of the Negro in Philadelphia," 260).

A century after Du Bois's *TPN* first appeared, the editors of the *Journal of Blacks in Higher Education* invited "some leading scholars" to comment on "how they view this work today." Amid several comments that *TPN* had been ignored over the years, William Julius Wilson wrote that although he would "argue that *TPN* is a pioneering study in sociological research," he also knew that it had been largely overlooked: "If students of sociology were asked to cite the trailblazing works of field research on urban race and ethnic relations, they would invariably mention studies published two decades or more later such as William I. Thomas and Florian Znaniecki's two-volume study (1918–20) *The Polish Peasant: Monograph of an Immigrant Group*, or Louis Wirth's (1928) *The Ghetto*, or Harvey W. Zorbaugh's (1929) *The Gold Coast and the Slum*." Those works, he said, were more likely to be taught, and even in 1998 "many students can go through their entire graduate program without being exposed to any of Du Bois' work, not to mention *The Philadelphia Negro*" (Wilson et al., "Du Bois' *The Philadelphia Negro*," 81).

13 Diedrich, "Review of *The Philadelphia Negro*," 531. Similarly, sociologist Elijah Anderson (in Wilson et al., "Du Bois' *The Philadelphia Negro*," 80) muses that "one can just imagine this stiff and proper Victorian gentleman in his suit and starched shirt moving through the hurly-burly of the noisy, congested neighborhood."

14 Diedrich, "Review of *The Philadelphia Negro*," 533.

15 Whyte, *Participant Observer*, 3.

16 Whyte, *Street Corner Society*, 72.

17 Whyte, 95.

18 Whyte, 120, 319.

19 Whyte, 126.

20 It also became the subject of a celebratory event at the Eastern Sociological Society in 1993 in conjunction with the fiftieth anniversary of its publication.

21 Frost et al., *Reframing Organizational Culture*.

22 Adler, Adler, and Johnson, "*Street Corner Society* Revisited."

23 Boelen, "*Street Corner Society*: Cornerville Revisited."

24 Whyte, "In Defense of *Street Corner Society*."

25 Denzin, "Whose Cornerville Is It, Anyway?"

26 Riley, in Frost et al., *Reframing Organizational Culture*, 218.

27 Richardson, "Trash on the Corner." Richardson would also like to see Whyte consider the ways in which his account rests on techniques of fiction and novel writing (making up dialogue; giving participants pseudonyms). And she adds she would like a deeper consideration of what is owed to "informants."

28 Whyte, "Revisiting *Street Corner Society*," 296–7.

29 Fox, *In the Field*, 1–2.

30 Fox, 2.

31 Fox, 86.

32 Fox, 89.

33 Fox, 89.

34 Fox, *Experiment Perilous*, 10.

35 Fox, 10.
36 Abel, *Living in Death's Shadow*, 4.
37 Nelson and Hertz, "On Being Open to Disruption," 1.

5. MEMOIRS AS EDUCATION

1 Frank, *Wounded Storyteller*.
2 For an argument that sociologists should approach stories from Frank's perspective of thinking "with" rather than "without," see Bochner and Ellis, *Evocative Autoethnography*.
3 For a discussion of the practice of using memoirs in the classroom, see Hartmann, "Personal Is Sociological"; Neustadter, "Significance of the Memoir Boom for Teaching Sociology," and Oslawski-Lopez, "Bringing Text to Life."
4 Of course memoirs are not the only supplemental material that can inspire the sociological imagination. Fiction, poetry, and movies have been used in classrooms with excellent results and for many of the same reasons. For discussions of using these other resources, see Carlin, "Corpus Status of Literature in Teaching Sociology"; Cosbey, "Using Contemporary Fiction to Teach Family Issues"; Fitzgerald, "Exploring Race in the Classroom"; Hartman, "Enriching Sociology 100"; Hegtvedt, "Teaching Sociology of Literature through Literature"; Hendershott and Wright, "Bringing the Sociological Perspective into the Interdisciplinary Classroom through Literature"; and Moran, "Versifying Your Reading List." Fitzgerald argues that fiction is preferable to memoir and autobiography for several reasons: fewer members of marginalized communities write memoirs than write fiction; concerns about veracity might be raised given the politics of publishing; and memoirs can be so idiosyncratic that they do not lend themselves to systematic analysis. Both fiction and nonfiction in the form of memoirs invite vicarious living, but, Fitzgerald argues, because novels are explicit about links between biography and history, they are more effective. With respect to poetry, Moran writes that while he agrees with the "advocates of the 'sociology through literature' approach in general," he believes that poetry can provide "many (if not all) of the benefits attributed to using literature, while carrying a few unique advantages over other genres." Moran, "Versifying Your Reading List," 121.
5 In a previous chapter I looked at memoirs that described becoming and then being sociologists. In this chapter I am more interested in those sociologists who narrate a set of discrete experiences (e.g., their childhood, an episode of illness) in the form of a memoir. Of course, no neat and tidy distinctions exist among various kinds of autobiographical writings by sociologists: to what one person calls a memoir, another might apply a vastly different label.
6 Conley, *Honky*.
7 For a discussion of whether or not this book constitutes sociology, see Marwell, "Review Essay."

8 See also Hartmann's "Personal Is Sociological" for a discussion of how this book has been used in the classroom as well as the discussion by Sternheimer, "Sociological Memoirs."

9 Kapitulik, "Race, Class, and Autobiography," 3.

10 Messner, *King of the Wild Suburb*.

11 Fried, *Caring for Red*.

12 Cohan, *Welcome to Wherever We Are*.

13 Cho, *Tastes Like War*.

14 Stein, *Boy's Journey*; Stein, "Biography, Trauma, the Holocaust and the Sociological Eye."

15 Wright, *Stardust to Stardust*.

16 Hendrickson, *Life on Delay*.

17 Robb, *Don't Think, Dear*.

18 Cunningham, *Sleeping Arrangements*.

19 Smith, "Standard North American Family."

20 Childers, *Welfare Brat*.

21 Jensen, *Carry*; Thomas, *Sink*; Eng, *Our Laundry, Our Town*.

22 Yousafzai and McCormick, *I Am Malala*; Oslawski-Lopez, "Bringing Text to Life."

23 Harger and Hallett, "Using *The Autobiography of Malcolm X* to Teach Introductory Sociology," 15; Malcolm X, *Autobiography of Malcolm X*.

24 Harger and Hallett, "Using *The Autobiography of Malcolm X* to Teach Introductory Sociology," 264.

25 On this issue, see, for example, the discussions in Carlin, "Corpus Status of Literature in Teaching Sociology," and Korgen, "Boy's Journey."

26 See, for example, Dimitrova, "Book Review"; Harger and Hallett, "Using *The Autobiography of Malcolm X* to Teach Introductory Sociology"; Hartmann, "Personal Is Sociological"; Inderbitzin, "Review of *Educated*"; Lewis, "Developing a Sociological Perspective on Mental Illness"; Mykoff, "Ordinary Lives"; Neustadter, "Significance of the Memoir Boom for Teaching Sociology"; Oslawski-Lopez, "Bringing Text to Life."

27 For a similar argument about fiction, see Hegtvedt, "Teaching Sociology of Literature through Literature." Hegtvedt reviews reasons for using literature in a classroom: providing examples of sociological concepts, illuminating social processes, creating opportunities to explore sociological content in new contexts, and learning how to apply structural analyses.

28 Mack and Alexander, "Ethics of Memoir," 51.

29 Vance, *Hillbilly Elegy*; Coates, *Between the World and Me*.

30 Gates, *Colored People*; hooks, *Bone Black*.

31 Stein, *Boy's Journey*, 278.

32 Cooper, *Better Living through Birding*.

33 Cosbey, "Using Contemporary Fiction to Teach Family Issues."

34 Lewis, "Developing a Sociological Perspective on Mental Illness."

35 Mykoff, "Ordinary Lives"; Neustadter, "Significance of the Memoir Boom for Teaching Sociology."

36 Lewis, "Developing a Sociological Perspective on Mental Illness"; Hartmann, "Personal Is Sociological."

37 Chang, "Autoethnography."

38 Harger and Hallett, "Using *The Autobiography of Malcolm X* to Teach Introductory Sociology."

39 Cosbey, "Using Contemporary Fiction to Teach Family Issues."

40 Korgen, "Boy's Journey"; Neustadter, "Significance of the Memoir Boom for Teaching Sociology."

41 Lewis, "Developing a Sociological Perspective on Mental Illness."

42 Harger and Hallett, "Using *The Autobiography of Malcolm X* to Teach Introductory Sociology."

43 For an interesting discussion, see Carlin, "Corpus Status of Literature in Teaching Sociology."

44 Mack and Alexander, "Ethics of Memoir."

45 Smith and Watson, *Reading Autobiography.*

46 For a good and open discussion of these issues, see Hodes, *My Hijacking.*

47 Eakin, *How Our Lives Become Stories.*

48 Oslawski-Lopez, "Bringing Text to Life."

49 Maynes, Pierce, and Laslett, *Telling Stories.*

50 Carlin, "Corpus Status of Literature in Teaching Sociology."

51 Butler, *Giving an Account of Oneself.*

52 Mack and Alexander, "Ethics of Memoir," 54.

53 Mack and Alexander, 67.

54 Oslawski-Lopez, "Bringing Text to Life."

55 De Bie, "Teaching with Madness," 40.

56 For a good discussion of these kinds of issues, see Whitlock, *Soft Weapons.*

6. MEMOIRS AS DATA

1 I focus here on sociological analyses. For a study by a historian, see Abel, *Living in Death's Shadow.* Among sociologists, Thomas DeGloma, in *Seeing the Light,* used memoirs for research along with other autobiographical accounts. See also, in disability studies, Apgar, *Disabled Child.* For shorter studies by sociologists that used published memoirs, see Carey, "Parents and Professionals"; Van der Kamp, Betten, and Krabbenborg, "In Their Own Words"; and Souza, "Intersections of 'Disability,' Gender, and Race." Judith Gerson, in "In Between States," uses unpublished memoirs for her analysis of Jewish identities.

2 Bjorklund, *Interpreting the Self.*

3 Goode, *Justifiable Conduct.*

4 Nelson, *Keeping Family Secrets.*

5 Frank, *Wounded Storyteller.*

6 Glaser and Strauss, *Discovery of Grounded Theory*, 168.

7 Maynes, Pierce, and Laslett, *Telling Stories*, 12.

8 For a thorough discussion of how to read autobiographies for social science analysis, see also Maynes, Pierce, and Laslett.

9 Bjorklund, *Interpreting the Self*.

10 For a fuller discussion of Bjorklund's sampling method, see her appendix A.

11 Bjorklund, *Interpreting the Self*, 13.

12 Bjorklund, 159.

13 Bjorklund, 17.

14 Bjorklund, 165.

15 Richardson, "Review of *Interpreting the Self*," 570.

16 Goode, *Justifiable Conduct*, locs. 50–52.

17 Goode, locs. 112–13.

18 Becker, *Outsiders*; Sykes and Matza, "Techniques of Neutralization."

19 Goode, *Justifiable Conduct*, locs. 359–61.

20 Goode, locs. 3068–70.

21 Goode, locs. 3088–89.

22 Nelson, *Keeping Family Secrets*.

23 Frank, *Wounded Storyteller*.

24 Frank, 77.

25 Frank, 97.

26 Frank, 115.

27 Frank, 158.

28 Maynes, Pierce, and Laslett, *Telling Stories*, 6.

29 See Amazon, "Adoption Memoirs" (n.d.), www.amazon.com; Goodreads, "Adoption Memoirs Books" (2024), www.goodreads.com; American Adoptions, "20 of the Best Adoptee Books Out There" (2024), www.americanadoptions. com.

30 Although a prior divorce might well have been a family secret during the 1950s, Nelson did not include that in her study because she could not find enough memoirs in which that had been a central issue. For an exception among memoirs, see Turkle, *Empathy Diaries*.

31 Calton, "Obscuring of Class in Memoirs of Parents of Children with Disabilities."

32 Carey, "Parents and Professionals."

33 Frank, *Wounded Storyteller*, 25.

34 Westover, *Educated*.

35 Childers, *Welfare Brat*.

36 Vance, *Hillbilly Elegy*.

37 Perry, *Friends, Lovers, and the Big Terrible Thing*.

38 Rivera, "I Am Mourning the Loss of Something I Loved."

39 For a more academic account of how social class position results in changing tastes, see Lareau, *Unequal Childhoods*.

40 Cotterill and Letherby, "Weaving Stories."
41 See, for example, Romero, *Maid's Daughter*, x.
42 Davis, "Rich Cases," 16.
43 Van der Kamp and colleagues ("In Their Own Words") asked permission of the men (or their families) before using their memoirs for their analysis of the experience of prostate cancer.

7. AUTOETHNOGRAPHY
 1 Pincus, "A Sociological Memoirist," 169–170.
 2 Merton, "Some Thoughts on the Concept of Sociological Autobiography," 18.
 3 Higgins and Johnson, *Personal Sociology*, 4. For a discussion of a reflexive approach, see Gouldner, *Coming Crisis of Western Sociology*.
 4 Becker, *Art Worlds*.
 5 Irwin, *Prisons in Turmoil*.
 6 Kanter, *Men and Women of the Corporation*.
 7 In 2022 Jeffrey Nash revived the term with essays on "Ringing the Cord: Sentimentality and Nostalgia among Male Singers" and "Laughter and Humor in the Classroom and Beyond," among others. Nash, *Personal Sociology*.
 8 Friedman, "Autobiographical Sociology," 61.
 9 The essays in Andersen and Zinn (discussed in chapter 3) do much of this. Many of the authors explain how their interest in, and analyses of, race and ethnicity derived from their firsthand experiences. See Andersen and Zinn, "Moving from the Margins."
10 Riley, *Sociological Lives*.
11 Shostak, *Private Sociology*, 8.
12 Evidence suggests that how readers view this style of researcher depends on their attitude toward the issue under investigation. According to Altenmüller, Lange, and Gollwitzer, "When participants hold favorable attitudes towards the research topic (i.e., LGBTQ or veganism), 'mesearchers' were perceived as more trustworthy and their research was perceived as more credible. This pattern was reversed when participants held unfavorable attitudes towards the research topic." In fact, the readers' attitudes shaped their perception of the entire field and not just a single study. Altenmüller, Lange, and Gollwitzer, "When Research Is Me-Search," 1.
13 Email from communications@asanet.org to the author, August 18, 2023.
14 Anderson and Glass-Coffin, "I Learn by Going"; Hayano, "Auto-ethnography."
15 Berger and Quinney, "Narrative Turn in Social Inquiry," 7.
16 Richardson, "Writing Sociology."
17 Adams, Ellis, and Jones, "Autoethnography."
18 McIlveen, "Autoethnography as a Method for Reflexive Research and Practice in Vocational Psychology."

19 Hayler, *Autoethnography, Self-Narrative and Teacher Education.*

20 Some commentators focus on the ways in which autoethnography is different from (and similar to) other ethnography rather than other forms of life writing, including memoir. See, for example, Anderson and Glass-Coffin, "I Learn by Going."

21 Poulos, *Essentials of Autoethnography*, 4. For another textbook with definitions, see Chang, "Autoethnography."

22 Anderson, "Analytic Autoethnography," 378.

23 Adams, "Autoethnographic Responsibilities."

24 Anderson did eventually backtrack on his assertion that analytic autoethnography was the only possible approach. In a piece co-authored by Bonnie Glass-Coffin, the authors argue that autoethnographic inquiry "integrates distinctive features of the 'new language of qualitative methods' . . . including the visibility of researcher's self, strong reflexivity, relational engagement, personal vulnerability, and open-ended rejection of finality and closure." See Anderson and Glass-Coffin, "I Learn by Going," 58. If, in the end, Anderson remains "committed to an analytic model of autoethnographic writing," he writes that he does so in 2014 "with a greater sense of blurred boundaries as opposed to clear distinctions." He continues, "In writing this chapter with Bonnie I've become convinced that the modes and key features of autoethnographic inquiry are similar no matter where along the spectrum from 'evocative' (e.g., Ellis, 1997) to 'analytic' (e.g., Anderson, 2006) one stands." Anderson and Glass-Coffin, 58.

25 Murphy, *Body Silent.*

26 Smith, "Analytic Autoethnography of Familial and Institutional Social Identity Construction."

27 Smith.

28 Nash, *Personal Sociology*, 13.

29 Atkinson, "Rescuing Autoethnography," 400.

30 Vryan, "Expanding Analytic Autoethnography and Enhancing Its Potential."

31 Charmaz, "Power of Names," 399.

32 Denzin, "Analytic Autoethnography," 423.

33 Bochner and Ellis, *Evocative Autoethnography*, 62–63.

34 Bochner and Ellis, 62–63.

35 Bochner and Ellis, 62–63.

36 Frank, *Wounded Storyteller.*

37 Bochner and Ellis, *Evocative Autoethnography*, 244.

38 Ellis, *Final Negotiations.*

39 Richardson, *Story of a Marriage through Dementia and Beyond*, 4.

40 Bloom, *In Love*; Fried, *Caring for Red*; Cohan, *Welcome to Wherever We Are.*

41 In their defense, Tony Adams refers to works like Richardson's *Story of a Marriage* and Ellis's *Final Negotiations* as offering "accessible, concrete, emotional, and

embodied accounts of personal and cultural experience." Adams,
"Autoethnographic Responsibilities."
42 Poulos, *Essentials of Autoethnography*.
43 Smith, "Analytic Autoethnography of Familial and Institutional Social Identity
Construction."
44 Bochner and Ellis, *Evocative Autoethnography*.
45 Boylorn and Orbe, *Critical Autoethnography*, 5.
46 Adams, "Autoethnographic Responsibilities," 64.
47 Dunn, *Talking White Trash*.
48 Poulos, *Essentials of Autoethnography*, 5.
49 Poulos, 5.
50 Chang, "Autoethnography," 52–53.

8. WRITING TO LEARN
1 For those who have found this kind of assignment useful, see Cook, "'To Actually
Be Sociological'"; Grauerholz and Copenhaver, "When the Personal Becomes
Problematic"; Kebede, "Practicing Sociological Imagination through Writing
Sociological Autobiography"; Powers, "Using Critical Autobiography to Teach the
Sociology of Education"; Ribbens, "Facts or Fictions?"; Ingram, "Teaching the
Sociology of Religion."
2 The full statement of this assignment is included as box 8.1.
3 Sometimes Nelson asked them to do this at the beginning of the semester; at that
time, they almost invariably focused on their own intelligence and hard work.
4 "Flash" usually denotes writing that is under 1,500 words, though often it's much
shorter, ranging from 200 to 1,000 words.
5 Armstrong, "Sick Role Memoir"; Ingram, "Teaching the Sociology of Religion";
Byczkowska-Owczarek and Jakubowska, "Sociology of the Body"; Powers, "Using
Critical Autobiography to Teach the Sociology of Education."
6 Cook, "'To Actually *Be* Sociological.'"
7 Kebede, "Practicing Sociological Imagination through Writing Sociological
Autobiography."
8 Mannon and Camfield, "Sociology Students as Storytellers."
9 Grauerholz and Copenhaver, "When the Personal Becomes Problematic."
10 Rebecca Tiger's mother died in November 2023, several months after she
completed this chapter.
11 Goffman, *Asylums*.
12 Tiger, "Zaftig."
13 Walker, "Braided Essay as Social Justice Action."

CONCLUSION
1 Stein, "Biography, Trauma, the Holocaust and the Sociological Eye"; Stein, *Boy's
Journey*; Simko, "Memoir and the Sociological Imagination," 271.

2 Abbott, "Against Narrative"; Pugh, "What Good Are Interviews for Thinking about Culture?"

3 Simko, "Memoir and the Sociological Imagination," 271. For a discussion linking history and memoir, in the sense of what they both do, see Hampl and May, "Introduction."

4 Maynes, Pierce, and Laslett, *Telling Stories.*

5 Frank, *Wounded Storyteller.*

6 Smith, "Analytic Autoethnography of Familial and Institutional Social Identity Construction," 3.

BIBLIOGRAPHY

Abbott, Andrew. "Against Narrative: A Preface to Lyrical Sociology." *Sociological Theory* 25, no. 1 (2007): 67–99. https://doi.org/10.1111/j.1467-9558.2007.00298.x.

Abel, Emily K. *Living in Death's Shadow: Family Experiences of Terminal Care and Irreplaceable Loss.* Baltimore: Johns Hopkins University Press, 2017.

Abel, Emily K., and Margaret K. Nelson. *The Farm & Wilderness Summer Camps: Progressive Ideals in the Twentieth Century.* New Brunswick, N.J.: Rutgers University Press, 2023.

———. *Limited Choices: Mable Jones, a Black Children's Nurse in a Northern White Household.* Charlottesville: University of Virginia Press, 2021.

Acker, Joan. "My Life as a Feminist Sociologist; or, Getting the Man Out of My Head." In Laslett and Thorne, *Feminist Sociology,* 28–47.

Adams, Lorraine. "Almost Famous: The Rise of the 'Nobody' Memoir." *Washington Monthly,* April 2002.

Adams, Tony E. "Autoethnographic Responsibilities." *International Review of Qualitative Research* 10, no. 1 (2017): 62–66.

Adams, Tony E., Carolyn Ellis, and Stacy Holman Jones. "Autoethnography." In *International Encyclopedia of Communication Research Methods.* New York: John Wiley, 2017. https://doi.org/10.1002/9781118901731.iecrm0011.

Adler, Patricia A., Peter Adler, and John M. Johnson. "*Street Corner Society* Revisited: New Questions about Old Issues." *Journal of Contemporary Ethnography* 21, no. 1 (1992): 3–10.

Ahlkvist, Jarl A. "Review of *A Misfit's Manifesto: The Spiritual Journey of a Rock & Roll Heart,* by Donna Gaines." *Teaching Sociology* 32, no. 2 (2004): 245–46.

Aikau, Hokulani K., Karla A. Erickson, and Jennifer L. Pierce, eds. *Feminist Waves, Feminist Generations: Life Stories from the Academy.* Minneapolis: University of Minnesota Press, 2007.

Albom, Mitch. *Tuesdays with Morrie: An Old Man, a Young Man, and Life's Greatest Lesson.* 25th anniv. ed. New York: Crown, 2007.

Allison, Dorothy. *Bastard Out of Carolina.* New York: Penguin, 2005.

Altenmüller, Marlene Sophie, Leonie Lucia Lange, and Mario Gollwitzer. "When Research Is Me-Search: How Researchers' Motivation to Pursue a Topic Affects

Laypeople's Trust in Science." *PLOS ONE* 16, no. 7 (2021): e0253911. https://doi. org/10.1371/journal.pone.0253911.

Andersen, Margaret L. "From Clueless to Critical: My Journey to Understanding the Intersections of Race, Class, and Gender." In Andersen and Zinn, *Moving from the Margins*, 40–50.

Andersen, Margaret L., and Maxine Baca Zinn, eds. *Moving from the Margins: Life Histories on Transforming the Study of Racism*. Stanford, Calif.: Stanford University Press, 2024.

———. "Moving from the Margins: Life Histories on Transforming the Study of Racism: An Introduction." In Andersen and Zinn, *Moving from the Margins*, 1–16.

Anderson, Leon. "Analytic Autoethnography." *Journal of Contemporary Ethnography* 35, no. 4 (2006): 373–95.

Anderson, Leon, and Bonnie Glass-Coffin. "I Learn by Going." In *Handbook of Autoethnography*. Routledge Handbooks Online, 2013. https://doi. org/10.4324/9781315427812.

Apgar, Amanda. *The Disabled Child: Memoirs of a Normal Future*. Ann Arbor: University of Michigan Press, 2023.

Armstrong, Elizabeth. "Sick Role Memoir." *TRAILS: Teaching Resources and Innovations Library for Sociology*, April 26, 2010. https://ojs.trails-asanet-org.aghosted. com.

Atkinson, Paul. "Narrative Turn or Blind Alley?" *Qualitative Health Research* 7, no. 3 (1997): 325–44.

———. "Rescuing Autoethnography." *Journal of Contemporary Ethnography* 35, no. 4 (2006): 400–404.

Babbie, Earl R. "An Accidental Career." Opportunities in Retirement Network Lecture, 2015. www.asanet.org.

———. *The Practice of Social Research*. 15th ed. Boston: Cengage, 2020.

Baldwin, Neil. *Martha Graham: When Dance Became Modern*. New York: Knopf, 2022.

Beam, Joseph. "Brother to Brother: Words from the Heart." In *In the Life: A Black Gay Anthology*, edited by Joseph Beam, 180–91. Washington, D.C.: RedBone Press, 1986.

Beaton, Kate. *Ducks: Two Years in the Oil Sands*. Montreal: Drawn & Quarterly, 2022.

Bechdel, Alison. *Fun Home: A Family Tragicomic*. Repr. ed. Boston: Mariner Books, 2007.

Becker, Howard S. *Art Worlds*. 25th anniv. ed. Berkeley: University of California Press, 2008.

———. *Outsiders: Studies in the Sociology of Deviance*. Repr. ed. New York: Free Press, 1966.

Becker, Matt. "The We in the Me: Memoir as Community." In Hampl and May, *Tell Me True*, locs. 1623–1821.

Bendix, Reinhard. *From Berlin to Berkeley: German-Jewish Identities*. New Brunswick, N.J.: Transaction, 1986.

Berger, Bennett M., ed. *Authors of Their Own Lives: Intellectual Autobiographies by Twenty American Sociologists*. Berkeley: University of California Press, 1992.

Berger, Peter L. *Adventures of an Accidental Sociologist: How to Explain the World without Becoming a Bore*. New York: Prometheus, 2011.

Berger, Ronald J., and Richard Quinney. "The Narrative Turn in Social Inquiry." In *Storytelling Sociology: Narrative as Social Inquiry*, edited by Ronald J. Berger and Richard Quinney, 1–12. Boulder, Colo: Lynne Rienner, 2004.

Bernard, Jessie. "A Woman's Twentieth Century." In Berger, *Authors of Their Own Lives*, 323–48.

Bessire, Lucas. *Running Out: In Search of Water on the High Plains*. Princeton, N.J.: Princeton University Press, 2021.

Beverley, John. "Testimonio, Subalternity, and Narrative Authority." In *A Companion to Latin American Literature and Culture*, edited by Sara Castro-Klarén, 571–83. New York: John Wiley, 2022.

Bjorklund, Diane. *Interpreting the Self: Two Hundred Years of American Autobiography*. Chicago: University of Chicago Press, 1999.

Bloom, Amy. *In Love: A Memoir of Love and Loss*. New York: Random House, 2022.

Bochner, Arthur, and Carolyn Ellis. *Evocative Autoethnography: Writing Lives and Telling Stories*. New York: Routledge, 2016.

Boelen, W. A. Marianne. "*Street Corner Society*: Cornerville Revisited." *Journal of Contemporary Ethnography* 21, no. 1 (1992): 11–51.

Booth, Percy N. "Review of *The Philadelphia Negro: A Social Study*, by W. E. Burghardt Du Bois." *Annals of the American Academy of Political and Social Science* 15 (1900): 100–102.

Boylorn, Robin M., and Mark P. Orbe, eds. *Critical Autoethnography: Intersecting Cultural Identities in Everyday Life*. 2nd ed. New York: Routledge, 2020.

Boynton, Graham. *Wild: The Life of Peter Beard: Photographer, Adventurer, Lover*. New York: St. Martin's, 2022.

Branch, Enobong Hannah. "Life Histories on Transforming the Study of Racism: An Introduction." In Andersen and Zinn, *Moving from the Margins*, 29–39.

Bruner, Jerome. "Life as Narrative." In Irvine, Pierce, and Zussman, *Narrative Sociology*, 121–36.

———. "The Narrative Creation of Self." In *The Handbook of Narrative and Psychotherapy: Practice, Theory, and Research*, edited by Lynne E. Angus and John McLeod, 3–14. Thousand Oaks, Calif.: Sage, 2004.

———. "Self-Making and World-Making." *Narrative and Identity: Studies in Autobiography, Self and Culture* 1 (2001): 25–37.

Buenavista, Tracy Lachica, Dimpal Jain, and María C. Ledesma, eds. *First-Generation Faculty of Color: Reflections on Research, Teaching, and Service*. New Brunswick, N.J.: Rutgers University Press, 2022.

Buss, Helen M., ed. *Repossessing the World: Reading Memoirs by Contemporary Women*. Waterloo, Ont.: Wilfrid Laurier University Press, 2002.

Butler, Judith. *Giving an Account of Oneself*. New York: Fordham University Press, 2005.

Byczkowska-Owczarek, Dominika, and Honorata Jakubowska. "Sociology of the Body—Teaching Embodied Approach through Autoethnography." *Qualitative Sociology Review* 14, no. 2 (2018): 152–64.

Caldwell, Gail. *Let's Take the Long Way Home: A Memoir of Friendship*. New York: Random House, 2010.

Calton, Cindee. "The Obscuring of Class in Memoirs of Parents of Children with Disabilities." *Disability & Society* 25, no. 7 (2010): 849–60. https://doi.org/10.1080/0968 7599.2010.520901.

Carey, Allison C. "Parents and Professionals." In *Disability Histories*, edited by Susan Burch and Michael Rembis, 58–76. Urbana: University of Illinois Press, 2014.

Carlin, Andrew P. "The Corpus Status of Literature in Teaching Sociology: Novels as 'Sociological Reconstruction.'" *American Sociologist* 41, no. 3 (2010): 211–31. https://doi.org/10.1007/s12108-010-9096-8.

Chang, Heewon. "Autoethnography." In *Autoethnography as Method*, 43–58. New York: Routledge, 2016.

Charmaz, Kathy. "The Power of Names." *Journal of Contemporary Ethnography* 35, no. 4 (2006): 396–99.

Chast, Roz. *Can't We Talk about Something More Pleasant? A Memoir*. Repr. ed. New York: Bloomsbury, 2016.

Chávez, Denise. *A Taco Testimony: Meditations on Family, Food and Culture*. Tucson, Ariz.: Rio Nuevo, 2006.

Childers, Mary. *Welfare Brat*. Repr. ed. New York: Bloomsbury, 2006.

Cho, Grace. *Tastes Like War: A Memoir*. New York: Feminist Press, 2021.

Coates, Ta-Nehisi. *Between the World and Me*. New York: One World, 2015.

Cohan, Deborah J. *Welcome to Wherever We Are: A Memoir of Family, Caregiving, and Redemption*. New Brunswick, N.J.: Rutgers University Press, 2020.

Colfer, Patrick. "Peter McHugh: A Memoir of the Passion of Theorizing." *Human Studies* 33, no. 2–3 (2010): 281–86. https://doi.org/10.1007/s10746-010-9152-y.

Collins, Patricia Hill. *Black Feminist Thought: Knowledge, Consciousness, and the Politics of Empowerment*. New York: Routledge, 2008.

Conley, Dalton. *Honky*. Berkeley: University of California Press, 2000.

Conway, Jill Ker. *The Road from Coorain*. New York: Knopf, 1989.

———. *When Memory Speaks*. Repr. ed. New York: Vintage, 1999.

Cook, Peta S. "'To Actually *Be* Sociological': Autoethnography as an Assessment and Learning Tool." *Journal of Sociology* 50, no. 3 (2014): 269–82.

Cooper, Christian. *Better Living through Birding: Notes from a Black Man in the Natural World*. New York: Random House, 2023.

Corona, Victor. *Night Class: A Downtown Memoir*. New York: Soft Skull, 2017.

Cosbey, Janet. "Using Contemporary Fiction to Teach Family Issues." *Teaching Sociology* 25, no. 3 (1997): 227–33. https://doi.org/10.2307/1319399.

Coser, Lewis A. *The Functions of Social Conflict: An Examination of the Concept of Social Conflict and Its Use in Empirical Sociological Research*. New York: Free Press, 1964.

———. "Notes on a Double Career." In Riley, *Sociological Lives*, 65–70.

Cotterill, Pamela, and Gayle Letherby. "Weaving Stories: Personal Auto/Biographies in Feminist Research." *Sociology* 27, no. 1 (1993): 67–79. https://doi.org/10.1177/0038038593027001007.

Cottom, Tressie McMillan. *Thick: And Other Essays*. New York: New Press, 2018.

Couser, G. Thomas. *Memoir: An Introduction*. Oxford: Oxford University Press, 2011.

Crenshaw, Kimberlé. "Mapping the Margins: Intersectionality, Identity Politics, and Violence Against Women of Color." *Stanford Law Review* 43 (1991): 1241–99.

Cunningham, Laura Shaine. *Sleeping Arrangements*. New York: Riverhead Books, 2000.

Daniels, Arlene Kaplan. "When We Were All Boys Together: Graduate School in the Fifties and Beyond." In Orlans and Wallace, *Gender and the Academic Experience*, 27–44.

Daniels, Jessie. *Nice White Ladies: The Truth about White Supremacy, Our Role in It, and How We Can Help Dismantle It*. New York: Seal Press, 2021.

Darling, Rosalyn Benjamin. "Introduction." In Darling and Stein, *Journeys in Sociology*, 1–6.

Darling, Rosalyn Benjamin, and Peter J. Stein, eds. *Journeys in Sociology: From First Encounters to Fulfilling Retirements*. Philadelphia: Temple University Press, 2017.

Davidman, Lynn. *Motherloss*. Berkeley: University of California Press, 2000.

Davis, Dena S. "Rich Cases: The Ethics of Thick Description." *Hastings Center Report* 21, no. 4 (1991): 12–17. https://doi.org/10.2307/3562994.

Davis, Katharine Bement. "The Condition of the Negro in Philadelphia." *Journal of Political Economy* 8, no. 2 (1900): 248–60. https://doi.org/10.1086/250661.

de Bie, Alise. "Teaching with Madness / 'Mental Illness' Autobiographies in Postsecondary Education: Ethical and Epistemological Implications." *Medical Humanities* 48, no. 1 (2022): 37–50. https://doi.org/10.1136/medhum-2020-011974.

DeGloma, Thomas. *Seeing the Light: The Social Logic of Personal Discovery*. Ill. ed. Chicago: University of Chicago Press, 2014.

Denzin, Norman K. "Analytic Autoethnography, or Déjà Vu All over Again." *Journal of Contemporary Ethnography* 35, no. 4 (2006): 419–28.

DeVault, Marjorie L. *Feeding the Family: The Social Organization of Caring as Gendered Work*. Repr. ed. Chicago: University of Chicago Press, 1994.

———. "A Second Generation Story." In Laslett and Thorne, *Feminist Sociology*, 257–74.

———. "Whose Cornerville Is It, Anyway?" *Journal of Contemporary Ethnography* 21, no. 1 (1992): 120–32.

Diedrich, Maria. "Review of *The Philadelphia Negro: A Social Study*, by W. E. B. Du Bois." *Amerikastudien / American Studies* 43, no. 3 (1998): 531–34.

Dill, Bonnie Thornton, "From the Sandbox." In Anderson and Zinn, *Moving from the Margins*, 108–120.

Dimitrova, Svetla. "Book Review: *Carry: A Memoir of Survival on Stolen Land*." *Teaching Sociology* 50, no. 2 (2022): 185–88. https://doi.org/10.1177/0092055X221084025.

Du Bois, W. E. B. *The Autobiography of W. E. B. Du Bois: A Soliloquy on Viewing My Life from the Last Decade of Its First Century*. Edited by Herbert Aptheker. 1962. New York: International, 1968.

———. *Darkwater: Voices from Within the Veil*. 1920. Mineola, N.Y.: Dover, 1999.

———. *Dusk of Dawn: An Essay toward an Autobiography of a Race Concept*. Edited by Henry Louis Gates Jr. and Kwame Anthony Appiah. 1940. Oxford: Oxford University Press, 2014.

———. *W. E. B. Du Bois on Sociology and the Black Community*. Chicago: University of Chicago Press, 1978.

Duneier, Mitchell. *Sidewalk*. New York: Farrar, Straus and Giroux, 2000.

Dunn, Tasha. *Talking White Trash: Mediated Representations and Lived Experiences of White Working-Class People*. New York: Routledge, 2018.

Eakin, Paul John. *How Our Lives Become Stories: Making Selves*. Ithaca, N.Y.: Cornell University Press, 1999.

Egan, David, and Kathleen Egan. *More Alike Than Different: My Life with Down Syndrome*. Guilford, Conn.: Prometheus, 2020.

Ellis, Carolyn. *Final Negotiations: A Story of Love, Loss, and Chronic Illness*. Rev. ed. Philadelphia: Temple University Press, 2018.

Eng, Alvin. *Our Laundry, Our Town: My Chinese American Life from Flushing to the Downtown Stage and Beyond*. New York: Empire State Editions, 2022.

Enninful, Edward. *A Visible Man: The First Black Editor in British* Vogue's *History*. New York: Bloomsbury, 2023.

Etzioni, Amitai. *My Brother's Keeper: A Memoir and a Message*. Ill. ed. Lanham, Md.: Rowman & Littlefield, 2003.

Ewick, Patricia, and Susan S. Silbey. "Subversive Stories and Hegemonic Tales: Toward a Sociology of Narrative." *Law & Society Review* 29, no. 2 (1995): 197–226. https://doi.org/10.2307/3054010.

Feyerabend, Paul. *Killing Time: The Autobiography of Paul Feyerabend*. Chicago: University of Chicago Press, 1996.

Fitzgerald, Charlotte D. "Exploring Race in the Classroom: Guidelines for Selecting the 'Right' Novel." *Teaching Sociology* 20, no. 3 (1992): 244–47. https://doi.org/10.2307/1319067.

Fox, Renée C. *Experiment Perilous: Physicians and Patients Facing the Unknown*. Repr. ed. 1959. New Brunswick, N.J.: Routledge, 1997.

———, ed. *In the Field: A Sociologist's Journey*. New Brunswick, N.J.: Routledge, 2011.

Frank, Arthur W. "Illness and Autobiographical Work: Dialogue as Narrative Destabilization." *Qualitative Sociology* 23, no. 1 (2000): 135–56.

———. *Letting Stories Breathe: A Socio-narratology*. Chicago: University of Chicago Press, 2010.

———. *The Wounded Storyteller: Body, Illness, and Ethics*. Chicago: University of Chicago Press, 1997.

Frey, James. *A Million Little Pieces*. New York: Anchor, 2003.

Fried, Mindy. *Caring for Red: A Daughter's Memoir*. Nashville: Vanderbilt University Press, 2016.

Friedman, Norman L. "Autobiographical Sociology." *American Sociologist* 21, no. 1 (1990): 60–66.

Frost, Peter J., Larry F. Moore, Meryl Reis Louis, Craig C. Lundberg, and Joanne Martin, eds. *Reframing Organizational Culture*. Newbury Park, Calif.: Sage, 1991.

Gaines, Donna. *A Misfit's Manifesto: The Sociological Memoir of a Rock & Roll Heart*. New Brunswick, N.J.: Rutgers University Press, 2007.

Garey, Anita Ilta, and Karen B. Hansen. *At the Heart of Work and Family: Engaging the Ideas of Arlie Hochschild*. New Brunswick, N.J.: Rutgers University Press, 2011.

Garner, Dwight. "Mary Karr." *Salon*, May 21, 1997. www.salon.com.

Gates, Henry Louis, Jr. *Colored People: A Memoir*. Repr. ed. New York: Vintage, 1995.

Genzlinger, Neil. "The Problem with Memoirs." *New York Times*, January 28, 2011, Books sec. www.nytimes.com.

Gerson, Judith M. "In Between States: National Identity Practices among German Jewish Immigrants." *Political Psychology* 22, no. 1 (2001): 179–98. https://doi.org/10.1111/0162-895X.00232.

———. "Review of *Feminist Sociology: Life Histories of a Movement*, by Barbara Laslett and Barrie Thorne, and *Fields of Play: Constructing an Academic Life*, by Laurel Richardson." *Signs* 26, no. 3 (2001): 911–14.

Glaser, Barney G., and Anselm L. Strauss. *The Discovery of Grounded Theory*. Chicago: Aldine, 1967.

Glenn, Evelyn Nakano. "Looking Back in Anger? Re-remembering My Sociological Career." In Laslett and Thorne, *Feminist Sociology*, 73–102.

Goertzel, Ted. "Albert Szymanski: A Personal and Political Memoir." *Critical Sociology* 15, no. 2 (1988): 139–44. https://doi.org/10.1177/089692058801500211.

Goetting, Ann. "Introduction: Fictions of the Self." In Goetting and Fenstermaker, *Individual Voices, Collective Visions*, 2–22.

Goetting, Ann, and Sarah Fenstermaker, eds. *Individual Voices, Collective Visions: Fifty Years of Women in Sociology*. Philadelphia: Temple University Press, 1995.

Goffman, Alice. *On the Run: Fugitive Life in an American City*. Repr. ed. New York: Picador, 2015.

Goffman, Erving. *Asylums: Essays on the Social Situation of Mental Patients and Other Inmates*. Garden City, N.Y.: Anchor, 1961.

Goode, Erich. *Justifiable Conduct: Self-Vindication in Memoir*. Philadelphia: Temple University Press, 2012.

Gopnik, Adam. "Annie Ernaux's Justly Deserved Nobel." *New Yorker*, October 9, 2022. www.newyorker.com.

Gordon-Reed, Annette. *On Juneteenth*. New York: Liveright, 2021.

Gouldner, Alvin W. *The Coming Crisis of Western Sociology*. New York: Basic Books, 1970.

Grandin, Greg. *Who Is Rigoberta Menchú?* Abr. ed. New York: Verso, 2011.

Grauerholz, Elizabeth, and Stacey Copenhaver. "When the Personal Becomes Problematic: The Ethics of Using Experiential Teaching Methods." *Teaching Sociology* 22, no. 4 (1994): 319–27. https://doi.org/10.2307/1318924.

Grealy, Lucy. *Autobiography of a Face*. Repr. ed. Boston: Mariner Books, 1994.

Greenhalgh, Susan. *Under the Medical Gaze: Facts and Fictions of Chronic Pain*. Berkeley: University of California Press, 2001.

Gutiérrez y Muhs, Gabriella, Yolanda Flores Niemann, Carmen G. González, Angela P. Harris, and Carmen G. Gonzalez, eds. *Presumed Incompetent: The Intersections of Race and Class for Women in Academia*. Denver: University Press of Colorado, 2012.

Hairston, Kimetta R., ed. *The Ivory Tower: Perspectives of Women of Color in Higher Education*. Lanham, Md.: Rowman & Littlefield, 2022.

Hall, Peter M. "The Sociological Consequences of Choosing Radical Parents: The Political, the Personal, and the Professional." in *Journeys in Sociology: From First Encounters to Fulfilling Retirements*, edited by Rosalyn Benjamin Darling and Peter J. Stein, 59–68. Philadelphia: Temple University Press, 2017.

Hampl, Patricia, and Elaine Tyler May. "Introduction." In Hampl and May, *Tell Me True*, locs. 53–114.

———, eds. *Tell Me True: Memoir, History, and Writing a Life*. Nepean, Ont.: Borealis Books.

Hansen, Karen V. *Encounter on the Great Plains: Scandinavian Settlers and the Dispossession of Dakota Indians, 1890–1930*. Repr. ed. Oxford: Oxford University Press, 2016.

Harger, Brent D., and Tim Hallett. "Using *The Autobiography of Malcolm X* to Teach Introductory Sociology." In *Teaching the Novel across the Curriculum: A Handbook for Educators*, ed. Colin C. Irvine, 259–71. Westport, Conn.: Greenwood, 2007.

Harris, Angela P. "Foreword: Presumed Incompetent in the Era of Diversity." In *Presumed Incompetent II: Race, Class, Power, and Resistance of Women in Academia*, edited by Yolanda Flores Niemann, Gabriella Gutiérrez y Muhs, and Carmen G. González, ix–x. Logan: Utah State University Press, 2020.

Harrison, Kathryn, and Jane Smiley. *The Kiss: A Memoir*. New York: Random House, 2011.

Hartman, Cheryl J. "Enriching Sociology 100: Using the Novel *Things Fall Apart*." *Teaching Sociology* 33, no. 3 (2005): 317–22. https://doi.org/10.1177/0092055X0503300312.

Hartmann, Doug. "The Personal Is Sociological." *Editors' Desk*, November 5, 2013. https://thesocietypages.org.

Hayano, David M. "Auto-ethnography: Paradigms, Problems, and Prospects." *Human Organization* 38, no. 1 (1979): 99–104.

Hayler, Mike. *Autoethnography, Self-Narrative and Teacher Education*. Vol. 5. New York: Springer, 2012.

Hegtvedt, Karen A. "Teaching Sociology of Literature through Literature." *Teaching Sociology* 19, no. 1 (1991): 1–12. https://doi.org/10.2307/1317567.

Hendershott, Anne, and Sheila Wright. "Bringing the Sociological Perspective into the Interdisciplinary Classroom through Literature." *Teaching Sociology* 21, no. 4 (1993): 325–31. https://doi.org/10.2307/1319081.

Henderson, George, and David W. Levy. *Race and the University: A Memoir*. Norman: University of Oklahoma Press, 2010.

Hendrickson, John. *Life on Delay: Making Peace with a Stutter*. New York: Knopf, 2023.

Hess, Beth. "An Accidental Sociologist." In Goetting and Fenstermaker, *Individual Voices, Collective Visions*, 37–50.

Higashida, Naoki. *The Reason I Jump: The Inner Voice of a Thirteen-Year-Old Boy with Autism*. Translated by K. A. Yoshida and David Mitchell. Repr. ed. New York: Random House, 2016.

Higginbotham, Elizabeth. "Networking across Stages of a Career." In Darling and Stein, *Journeys in Sociology*, 186–96.

Higgins, Paul C., and John M. Johnson, eds. *Personal Sociology*. New York: Praeger, 1988.

Hill, Jemele. *Uphill: A Memoir*. New York: Henry Holt, 2022.

Hochschild, Arlie Russell. "Inside the Clockwork of Male Careers." In Orlans and Wallace, *Gender and the Academic Experience*, 125–40.

Hodes, Martha. *My Hijacking: A Personal History of Forgetting and Remembering*. New York: Harper, 2023.

Homans, George Caspar. *Coming to My Senses: The Autobiography of a Sociologist*. New Brunswick, N.J.: Routledge, 2013.

Hondagneu-Sotelo, Pierrette. *Domestica: Immigrant Workers Cleaning and Caring in the Shadows of Affluence*. Berkeley: University of California Press, 2007.

———. "Shifting Boundaries." In Andersen and Zinn, *Moving from the Margins*, 132–41.

hooks, bell. *Bone Black: Memories of Girlhood*. Repr. ed. New York: Henry Holt, 1997.

Hsu, Hua. *Stay True: A Memoir*. New York: Doubleday, 2022.

Hunter, Marcus A., ed. *The New Black Sociologists: Historical and Contemporary Perspectives*. New York: Routledge, 2018.

Inderbitzin, Michelle. "Review of *Educated*, by Tara Westover." *Teaching Sociology* 48, no. 2 (2020): 158–60.

Ingram, Larry C. "Teaching the Sociology of Religion: The Student's Religious Autobiography." *Teaching Sociology* 6, no. 2 (1979): 161–71. https://doi.org/10.2307/1317264.

Irvine, Leslie J., Jennifer L. Pierce, and Robert Zussman, eds. *Narrative Sociology.* Nashville: Vanderbilt University Press, 2019.

Irwin, John. *Prisons in Turmoil.* 3rd ed. Boston: Little, Brown, 1980.

Jelinek, Estelle C. "Teaching Women's Autobiographies." *College English* 38, no. 1 (1976): 32–45. https://doi.org/10.2307/375986.

Jensen, Toni. *Carry: A Memoir of Survival on Stolen Land.* New York: Ballantine Books, 2020.

Johnson, Fenton. *Geography of the Heart.* Repr. ed. New York: Scribner, 1997.

———. "The Lion and the Lamb, or the Facts and the Truth: Memoir as Bridge." In Hampl and May, *Tell Me True,* locs. 119–334.

Johnson, Nina A. "For, By and About: Notes on a Sociology of Black Liberation." In Hunter, *New Black Sociologists,* 149–62.

Kakutani, Michiko. *The Death of Truth: Notes on Falsehood in the Age of Trump.* Repr. ed. New York: Crown, 2019.

Kanter, Rosabeth Moss. *Men and Women of the Corporation.* New ed. New York: Basic Books, 2008.

Kapitulik, Brian. "Race, Class, and Autobiography: Exercising the Sociological Imagination." *TRAILS: Teaching Resources and Innovations Library for Sociology,* April 26, 2010. https://trails.asanet.org.

Kaplan, Alice. *French Lessons: A Memoir.* Chicago: University of Chicago Press, 2018.

———. "Lady of the Lake." In Hampl and May, *Tell Me True,* locs. 1340–1622.

Karr, Mary. *The Art of Memoir.* Repr. ed. New York: Harper, 2016.

———. *The Liars' Club: A Memoir.* Repr. ed. New York: Penguin, 2005.

Kavanagh, Jennifer, and Michael D. Rich. *Truth Decay: An Initial Exploration of the Diminishing Role of Facts and Analysis in American Public Life.* Santa Monica, Calif.: RAND, 2018.

Kebede, Alem. "Practicing Sociological Imagination through Writing Sociological Autobiography." *Teaching Sociology* 37, no. 4 (2009): 353–68. https://doi.org/10.1177/0092055X0903700404.

Kimball, Margaret. *And Now I Spill the Family Secrets: An Illustrated Memoir.* Ill. ed. New York: Harper, 2021.

Kingsley, Jason, and Mitchell Levitz. *Count Us In: Growing Up with Down Syndrome.* New York: Harper, 2007.

Korgen, Kathleen Odell. "A Boy's Journey: Public Sociology for In and Out of the Classroom." *Sociological Forum* 36, no. 1 (2021): 277–79. https://doi.org/10.1111/socf.12673.

Krakauer, Jon. *Three Cups of Deceit: How Greg Mortenson, Humanitarian Hero, Lost His Way.* New York: Anchor, 2011.

Kuchler, Susanne. *Images of Memory.* Edited by Walter Melion. Washington, D.C.: Smithsonian Institution, 1991.

Kupfer, Fern. *Before and After Zachariah.* Chicago: Chicago Review Press, 1998.

Lareau, Annette. *Unequal Childhoods: Class, Race, and Family Life.* Berkeley: University of California Press, 2003.

Larson, Thomas. *The Memoir and the Memoirist: Reading and Writing Personal Narrative.* Athens, Ohio: Swallow Press, 2007.

Laslett, Barbara, and Barrie Thorne, eds. *Feminist Sociology: Life Histories of a Movement.* New Brunswick, N.J.: Rutgers University Press, 1997.

———. "Life Histories of a Movement: An Introduction." In Laslett and Thorne, *Feminist Sociology,* 1–27.

Latina Feminist Group. *Telling to Live: Latina Feminist Testimonios.* Ill. ed. Durham, N.C.: Duke University Press, 2001.

Lazarsfeld, Paul F. "An Episode in the History of Social Research: A Memoir." *Perspectives in American History* 2 (1968): 270–337.

Lejeune, Philippe. "From Autobiography to Life-Writing, from Academia to Association: A Scholar's Story." Plenary lecture, Lexington, Ky., 2005. Translated by Marie-Danielle Leruez. www.autopacte.org.

Lerum, Kari. "What's Love Got to Do with It? Life Lessons from Multiracial Feminism." In Gutiérrez y Muhs et al., *Presumed Incompetent,* 266–76.

Lewis, Michael. "Developing a Sociological Perspective on Mental Illness through Reading Narratives and Active Learning: A 'Book Club' Strategy." *Teaching Sociology* 32, no. 4 (2004): 391–400. https://doi.org/10.1177/0092055X0403200405.

Lipset, Seymour Martin. "Steady Work: An Academic Memoir." *Annual Review of Sociology* 22 (1996): 1–27. www.jstor.org/stable/2083422.

Mack, Katherine, and Jonathan Alexander. "The Ethics of Memoir: *Ethos* in Uptake." *Rhetoric Society Quarterly* 49, no. 1 (2019): 49–70. https://doi.org/10.1080/02773945.2018.1546889.

Malcolm X. *The Autobiography of Malcolm X (as Told to Alex Haley).* Reissue ed. New York: Ballantine Books, 1992.

Manning, Chelsea. *README.txt: A Memoir.* New York: Farrar, Straus and Giroux, 2022.

Mannon, Susan E., and Eileen K. Camfield. "Sociology Students as Storytellers: What Narrative Sociology and C. Wright Mills Can Teach Us about Writing in the Discipline." *Teaching Sociology* 47, no. 3 (2019): 177–90. https://doi.org/10.1177/0092055X19828802.

Martindale, Don. *The Romance of a Profession: A Case History in the Sociology of Sociology.* 2nd ed. New Delhi: Intercontinental Press, 1986.

Marwell, Nicole P. "Review Essay: Sociological Uses of a Sociological Memoir." *Qualitative Sociology* 25, no. 1 (2002): 139–43. https://doi.org/10.1023/A:1014320727648.

Mason, Mary Ann, Nicholas H. Wolfinger, and Marc Goulden. *Do Babies Matter? Gender and Family in the Ivory Tower.* New Brunswick, N.J.: Rutgers University Press, 2013.

May, Elaine Tyler. "Confessions of a Memoir Thief." In Hampl and May, *Tell Me True*, locs. 1145–1339.

Maynes, Mary Jo, Jennifer L. Pierce, and Barbara Laslett. *Telling Stories: The Use of Personal Narratives in the Social Sciences and History*. Ithaca, N.Y.: Cornell University Press, 2012.

McCurdy, Jennette. *I'm Glad My Mom Died*. New York: Simon & Schuster, 2022.

McIlveen, Peter. "Autoethnography as a Method for Reflexive Research and Practice in Vocational Psychology." *Australian Journal of Career Development* 17, no. 2 (2008): 13–20.

Menchú, Rigoberta. *I, Rigoberta Menchú: An Indian Woman in Guatemala*. Edited by Elisabeth Burgos-Debray, translated by Ann Wright. 2nd ed. New York: Verso, 2010.

Mendelsohn, Daniel. "But Enough about Me." *New Yorker*, January 17, 2010. www.newyorker.com.

———. *An Odyssey: A Father, a Son, and an Epic*. New York: Vintage, 2017.

Merla, Patrick, ed. *Boys Like Us: Gay Writers Tell Their Coming Out Stories*. New York: Avon Books, 1996.

Merton, Robert K. "Some Thoughts on the Concept of Sociological Autobiography." In Riley, *Sociological Lives*, 17–22.

Messner, Michael A. *King of the Wild Suburb: A Memoir of Fathers, Sons and Guns*. Austin, Tex.: Plain View Press, 2011.

Miller, Nancy K. "But Enough about Me, What Do You Think of My Memoir?" *Yale Journal of Criticism* 13, no. 2 (2000): 421–36. https://doi.org/10.1353/yale.2000.0023.

———. *But Enough about Me: Why We Read Other People's Lives*. New York: Columbia University Press, 2022.

Mills, C. Wright. *The Sociological Imagination*. New York: Oxford University Press, 1959.

Mitchell, Wendy. *Somebody I Used to Know: A Memoir*. New York: Ballantine Books, 2018.

Moehringer, J. R. "Notes from Prince Harry's Ghostwriter." *New Yorker*, May 8, 2023. www.newyorker.com.

Moody, Anne. *Coming of Age in Mississippi: The Classic Autobiography of a Young Black Girl in the Rural South*. Repr. ed. New York: Delta, 2004.

Moore, Wendy Leo. "'I Thought She Was One of Us!': A Narrative Examination of Power and Exclusion in the Academy." In Aikau, Erickson, and Pierce, *Feminist Waves, Feminist Generations*, 250–69.

Moran, Timothy Patrick. "Versifying Your Reading List: Using Poetry to Teach Inequality." *Teaching Sociology* 27, no. 2 (1999): 110–25. https://doi.org/10.2307/1318698.

Mortenson, Greg, and David Oliver Relin. *Three Cups of Tea: One Man's Mission to Promote Peace—One School at a Time*. London: Penguin, 2007.

Murphy, Robert F. *The Body Silent: The Different World of the Disabled*. New York: Norton, 2001.

Myers, Leah. *Thinning Blood: A Memoir of Family, Myth, and Identity*. New York: Norton, 2023.

Mykoff, Nancy. "Ordinary Lives: Teaching History with Life Narratives in Transnational Perspective." In *Unhinging the National Framework: Perspectives on Transnational Life Writing*, edited by Babs Boter, Marleen Rensen, and Giles Scott-Smith, 145–62. Leiden: Sidestone Press, 2020.

Nash, Jeffrey E. *Personal Sociology: Finding Meanings in Everyday Life*. Lanham, Md.: Lexington Books, 2022.

Nazeer, Kamran. *Send in the Idiots: Stories from the Other Side of Autism*. New York: Bloomsbury, 2008.

Nelson, Margaret K. *Keeping Family Secrets: Shame and Silence in Memoirs from the 1950s*. New York: New York University Press, 2022.

Nelson, Margaret K., and Rosanna Hertz. "On Being Open to Disruption." In *Open to Disruption: Time and Craft in the Practice of Slow Sociology*, edited by Anita Ilta Garey, Rosanna Hertz, and Margaret K. Nelson, 1–22. Nashville: Vanderbilt University Press, 2014.

Neustadter, Roger. "The Significance of the Memoir Boom for Teaching Sociology." *Free Inquiry in Creative Sociology* 27, no. 2 (1999): 67–72.

Newman, Paul, and Melissa Newman. *The Extraordinary Life of an Ordinary Man: A Memoir*. Edited by David Rosenthal. New York: Vintage, 2022.

Obama, Michelle. *Becoming*. New York: Crown, 2018.

Olick, Jeffrey K. "'Collective Memory': A Memoir and Prospect." *Memory Studies* 1, no. 1 (2008): 23–29.

Olsen, Gregg. *If You Tell: A True Story of Murder, Family Secrets, and the Unbreakable Bond of Sisterhood*. Seattle: Thomas & Mercer, 2019.

Omi, Michael. "Thinking through Race." In Andersen and Zinn, *Moving from the Margins*, 51–61.

Orlans, Kathryn P. Meadow, and Ruth A. Wallace, eds. *Gender and the Academic Experience: Berkeley Women Sociologists*. Lincoln: University of Nebraska Press, 1994.

Oslawski-Lopez, Jamie. "Bringing Text to Life: Enhancing Introduction to Sociology with the Memoir 'I Am Malala.'" *TRAILS: Teaching Resources and Innovations Library for Sociology*, January 23, 2020. https://ojs.trails-asanet-org.aghosted.com.

Page, Charles. *Fifty Years in the Sociological Enterprise: A Lucky Journey*. Amherst: University of Massachusetts Press, 1985.

Perez, Domino Renee, and Norma E. Cantú. "Talking Testimonio: Telling History and Memory." *Journal of American Folklore* 135, no. 536 (2022): 150–63, 262, 264.

Perry, Matthew. *Friends, Lovers, and the Big Terrible Thing: A Memoir*. New York: Flatiron Books, 2022.

Pierce, Jennifer L. "Traveling from Feminism to Mainstream Sociology and Back: One Woman's Tale of Tenure and the Politics of Backlash." *Qualitative Sociology* 26, no. 3 (2003): 369–96. https://doi.org/10.1023/A:1024070310729.

Pincus, Fred L. "A Sociological Memoirist." In Darling and Stein, *Journeys in Sociology*, 160–170.

Polkinghorne, David. "Explanatory Narrative Research." In Irvine, Pierce, and Zussman, *Narrative Sociology*, 71–81.

Polletta, Francesca. "'It Was Like a Fever . . .': Narrative and Identity in Social Protest." In Irvine, Pierce, and Zussman, *Narrative Sociology*, 301–16.

Polletta, Francesca, Pang Ching Bobby Chen, Beth Gharrity Gardner, and Alice Motes. "The Sociology of Storytelling." *Annual Review of Sociology* 37, no. 1 (2011): 109–30. https://doi.org/10.1146/annurev-soc-081309-150106.

Poulos, Christopher N. *Essentials of Autoethnography*. Washington, D.C.: American Psychological Association, 2021.

Powers, Rosemary F. "Using Critical Autobiography to Teach the Sociology of Education." *Teaching Sociology* 26, no. 3 (1998): 198–206. https://doi.org/10.2307/1318833.

Preston, John. *A Member of the Family*. New York: Dutton Adult, 1992.

Pugh, Allison J. "What Good Are Interviews for Thinking about Culture? Demystifying Interpretive Analysis." *American Journal of Cultural Sociology* 1, no. 1 (2013): 42–68. https://doi.org/10.1057/ajcs.2012.4.

Rabin, Nathan. "Stephen Colbert." *AV Club*, January 25, 2006. www.avclub.com.

Rak, Julie. *Boom! Manufacturing Memoir for the Popular Market*. Ill. ed. Waterloo, Ont.: Wilfrid Laurier University Press, 2013.

———. "Memoir, Truthiness, and the Power of Oprah: The James Frey Controversy Reconsidered." *Prose Studies* 34, no. 3 (2012): 224–42. https://doi.org/10.1080/01440 357.2012.751260.

Revels, Alyssa. "Talking Tacos: Borderlands Culinary Rhetoric in a Taco Testimony." *Western American Literature* 57, no. 2 (2022): 99–109. https://doi.org/10.1353/ wal.2022.0003.

Reyes, Kathryn Blackmer, and Julia E. Curry Rodríguez. "Testimonio: Origins, Terms, and Resources." *Equity & Excellence in Education* 45, no. 3 (2012): 525–38.

Reyes, Victoria. *Academic Outsider: Stories of Exclusion and Hope*. Stanford, Calif.: Stanford University Press, 2022.

Ribbens, Jane. "Facts or Fictions? Aspects of the Use of Autobiographical Writing in Undergraduate Sociology." *Sociology* 27, no. 1 (1993): 81–92.

Richardson, Laurel. "Review of *Interpreting the Self: Two Hundred Years of American Autobiography*, by Diane Bjorklund." *Contemporary Sociology* 28, no. 5 (1999): 570–71. https://doi.org/10.2307/2655016.

———. *A Story of a Marriage through Dementia and Beyond: Love in a Whirlwind*. New York: Routledge, 2022.

———. "Trash on the Corner: Ethics and Technography." *Journal of Contemporary Ethnography* 21, no. 1 (1992): 103–19.

———. "Writing Sociology." *Cultural Studies ↔ Critical Methodologies* 2, no. 3 (2002): 414–22. https://doi.org/10.1177/153270860200200311.

Rickman, Alan. *Madly, Deeply: The Diaries of Alan Rickman*. New York: Henry Holt, 2022.

Riesman, David. "On Discovering and Teaching Sociology: A Memoir." *Annual Review of Sociology* 14 (1988): 1–25.

Riley, Matilda White, ed. *Sociological Lives: Social Change and the Life Course*. Vol. 2. Newbury Park, Calif.: Sage, 1988.

Rios, Victor M. *Punished: Policing the Lives of Black and Latino Boys*. New York: New York University Press, 2011.

Rivera, Adrian J. "I Am Mourning the Loss of Something I Loved: McNuggets." *New York Times*, February 28, 2023, Opinion sec. www.nytimes.com.

Robb, Alice. *Don't Think, Dear: On Loving and Leaving Ballet*. Boston: Mariner Books, 2023.

Robinson, Brandon Andrew. "Non-binary Embodiment, Queer Knowledge Production, and Disrupting the Cisnormative Field: Notes from a Trans Ethnographer." *Journal of Men's Studies* 30, no. 3 (2022): 425–45. https://doi.org/10.1177/10608265221108204.

Romero, Mary. "A Critical Race Feminist at the Crossroads of Biography and History." In Andersen and Zinn, *Moving from the Margins*, 86–96.

———. *Maid in the USA*. 10th anniv. ed. New York: Routledge, 2016.

———. *The Maid's Daughter: Living Inside and Outside the American Dream*. New York: New York University Press, 2011.

Rossi, Alice S. *Seasons of a Woman's Life: A Self-Reflective Essay on Love and Work in Family, Profession, and Politics*. Amherst: University of Massachusetts Press, 1983.

Rothman, Barbara Katz. *Weaving a Family: Untangling Race and Adoption*. Edited by William Loren Katz. Boston: Beacon, 2005.

———. "Writing Ourselves in Sociology." *Methodological Innovations Online* 2, no. 1 (2007): 11–16. https://doi.org/10.4256/mio.2007.0003.

Samatar, Sofia. *The White Mosque: A Memoir*. New York: Catapult, 2022.

Segura, Denise. "I Change Myself; I Change the World." In Andersen and Zinn, *Moving from the Margins*, 72–85.

Sehee, Baek. *I Want to Die but I Want to Eat Tteokbokki: A Memoir*. Translated by Anton Hur. Unabr. ed. New York: Bloomsbury, 2022.

Shostak, Arthur B., ed. *Private Sociology: Unsparing Reflections, Uncommon Gains*. Annotated ed. Lanham, Md.: Rowman & Littlefield, 1996.

Simko, Christina. "Memoir and the Sociological Imagination." *Sociological Forum* 36, no. 1 (2021): 271–76. https://doi.org/10.1111/socf.12672.

Simon, David R. "Spreading the Sociological Imagination to Lay Audiences." In Darling and Stein, *Journeys in Sociology*, 181–85.

Smith, Dorothy E. "A Berkeley Education." In Orlans and Wallace, *Gender and the Academic Experience*, 45–56.

———. *The Everyday World as Problematic: A Feminist Sociology*. Boston: Northeastern University Press, 1989.

———. "The Standard North American Family: SNAF as an Ideological Code." *Journal of Family Issues* 14 (1993): 50–65.

Smith, Michael J. *Black Men / White Men: A Gay Anthology.* San Francisco: Gay Sunshine Press, 1983.

Smith, Patrick. "What Memoir Forgets." *The Nation,* July 27, 1998.

Smith, Robert Courtney. "Analytic Autoethnography of Familial and Institutional Social Identity Construction of My Dad with Alzheimer's: In the Emergency Room with Erving Goffman and Oliver Sacks." *Social Science & Medicine* 277 (2021): 113894.

Smith, Sidonie, and Julia Watson. *Reading Autobiography: A Guide for Interpreting Life Narratives.* Minneapolis: University of Minnesota Press, 2010.

Snyder, Justin. "Review of *Seeing the Light: The Social Logic of Personal Discovery,* by Thomas DeGloma." *Qualitative Sociology Review* 12, no. 2 (2016): 124–26. https://doi.org/10.18778/1733-8077.12.2.07.

Souza, Cheryl Najarian. "Intersections of 'Disability,' Gender, and Race: The Deaf Community, Blindness, and DeafBlind Activism in Families." Manuscript, 2022.

Stacey, Judith. "Disloyal to the Disciplines: A Feminist Trajectory in the Borderlands." In Laslett and Thorne, *Feminist Sociology,* 126–50.

Stanfield, John H., ed. *A History of Race Relations Research: First Generation Recollections.* Newbury Park, Calif.: Sage, 1993.

Stein, Peter J. "Biography, Trauma, the Holocaust and the Sociological Eye." *Sociological Forum* 35, no. 4 (2020): 1337–45. https://doi.org/10.1111/socf.12650.

———. *A Boy's Journey: From Nazi-Occupied Prague to Freedom in America.* Chapel Hill, N.C.: Lystra, 2019.

———. "Conclusion." In Darling and Stein, *Journeys in Sociology,* 206–218.

Sternheimer, Karen. "Sociological Memoirs." *Everyday Sociology Blog,* June 13, 2011. www.everydaysociologyblog.com.

Stoll, David. *Rigoberta Menchú and the Story of All Poor Guatemalans.* New York: Routledge, 2019.

Sykes, Gresham M., and David Matza. "Techniques of Neutralization: A Theory of Delinquency." *American Sociological Review* 22, no. 6 (1957): 664–70.

Thomas, Joseph Earl. *Sink: A Memoir.* New York: Grand Central, 2023.

Tiger, Rebecca. *Judging Addicts: Drug Courts and Coercion in the Justice System.* New York: New York University Press, 2013.

———. "Zaftig." *Bending Genres,* no. 24 (2023). https://bendinggenres.com/zafting/.

Toews, Miriam. *Swing Low: A Life.* Repr. ed. New York: Harper, 2011.

Turkle, Sherry. *The Empathy Diaries: A Memoir.* New York: Penguin, 2021.

Turner, Stephen. *Mad Hazard: A Life in Social Theory.* Bingley, UK: Emerald, 2022.

Valentine, Sarah. *When I Was White: A Memoir.* Ill. ed. New York: St. Martin's, 2019.

Valverde, Kieu Linh Caroline, and Wei Ming Dariotis, eds. *Fight the Tower: Asian American Women Scholars' Resistance and Renewal in the Academy.* New Brunswick, N.J.: Rutgers University Press, 2019.

Vance, J. D. *Hillbilly Elegy: A Memoir of a Family and Culture in Crisis.* Repr. ed. New York: Harper, 2016.

van der Kamp, Jill, Afke Wieke Betten, and Lotte Krabbenborg. "In Their Own Words: A Narrative Analysis of Illness Memoirs Written by Men with Prostate Cancer." *Sociology of Health & Illness* 44, no. 1 (2022): 236–52.

Vaughan, Diane. *The Challenger Launch Decision: Risky Technology, Culture, and Deviance at NASA.* Chicago: University of Chicago Press, 1997.

Vryan, Kevin D. "Expanding Analytic Autoethnography and Enhancing Its Potential." *Journal of Contemporary Ethnography* 35, no. 4 (2006): 405–9.

Walker, Nicole. "The Braided Essay as Social Justice Action." *Creative Nonfiction,* no. 64 (2017): 6–12.

Wenner, Jann S. *Like a Rolling Stone: A Memoir.* Boston: Little, Brown, 2022.

Westover, Tara. *Educated: A Memoir.* New York: Random House, 2018.

Whitlock, Gillian. *Soft Weapons: Autobiography in Transit.* Chicago: University of Chicago Press, 2010.

Whyte, William Foote. "In Defense of *Street Corner Society." Journal of Contemporary Ethnography* 21 (1992): 52–68.

——. "Revisiting *Street Corner Society." Sociological Forum* 21, no. 1 (1992): 285–98.

——. *Participant Observer: An Autobiography.* Ithaca, N.Y.: Cornell University Press, 1994.

——. *Street Corner Society: Social Structure of an Italian Slum.* Enl. ed. Chicago: University of Chicago Press, 1955.

Williams, Donna. *Nobody Nowhere: The Remarkable Autobiography of an Autistic Girl.* New ed. London: Jessica Kingsley, 1998.

Williams, John, Joumana Khatib, Elizabeth A. Harris, and Alexandra Alter. "15 Memoirs and Biographies to Read This Fall." *New York Times,* September 8, 2022, Books sec. www.nytimes.com.

Willie, Charles Vert. "Commentary on Sociological Lives." In Riley, *Sociological Lives,* 163–76.

Wilson, William Julius, Gerald Early, David Levering Lewis, Elijah Anderson, James E. Blackwell, Ronald Walters, and Chuck Stone. "Du Bois' *The Philadelphia Negro*: 100 Years Later." *Journal of Blacks in Higher Education,* no. 11 (1996): 78–84. https://doi.org/10.2307/2963323.

Wingfield, Adia Harvey. "School Daze: Patricia Hill Collins, a College Classroom, and a New Sociology of Race." In Hunter, *New Black Sociologists,* 101–12.

Worsley, Lucy. *Agatha Christie: An Elusive Woman.* New York: Pegasus, 2022.

Wright, Erik Olin. *Stardust to Stardust: Reflections on Living and Dying.* Ill. ed. Chicago: Haymarket Books, 2020.

Wrong, Dennis. "Imagining the Real." In Berger, *Authors of Their Own Lives,* 3–22.

Yagoda, Ben. *Memoir: A History.* New York: Riverhead, 2009.

Young, Molly. "It's My Privilege: Glorious Memoirs by the Very Rich." *New York Times,* December 14, 2023, Books sec. www.nytimes.com.

Yousafzai, Malala, and Patricia McCormick. *I Am Malala: How One Girl Stood Up for Education and Changed the World.* Ill. ed. New York: Little, Brown, 2016.

Zamora, Javier. *Solito: A Memoir*. London: Hogarth, 2022.

Zhou, Min. *The Accidental Sociologist in Asian American Studies*. Edited by Russell C. Leong and Don T. Nakanishi. Los Angeles: UCLA Asian American Studies Center Press, 2011.

Zubrzycki, Jerzy. "Edward Shils—A Personal Memoir." *Quadrant* 40, no. 1–2 (1996): 61–63.

Zussman, Robert. "Autobiographical Occasions." *Contemporary Sociology* 25, no. 2 (1996): 143–48. https://doi.org/10.2307/2077159.

———. "Autobiographical Occasions: Introduction to the Special Issue." *Qualitative Sociology* 23 (2000): 5–8.

———. "A Boy's Journey and the Journey to Freedom." *Sociological Forum* 36, no. 1 (2021): 280–84. https://doi.org/10.1111/socf.12674.

———. "Picturing the Self: My Mother's Family Photo Albums." *Contexts* 5, no. 4 (2006): 28–34.

INDEX

Abel, Emily K., 2, 78
academia: patriarchy in, 61–62; racism in, 62
Acker, Joan, 54
activism, 50
Adams, Lorraine, 16
Adams, Tony, 128
addiction: Frey's scandal about, 37, 39, 40; of McCurdy, 2; of Perry, 2, 109
Adler, Patricia, 72
Adler, Peter, 72
adoption, 106
African American community, 54–56, 66, 67–68
agency, of memoir writers, 25
AI. *See* artificial intelligence
Albom, Mitch, 5
Alexander, Jonathan, 41
alienation, 52
Allison, Dorothy, 4
Altenmüller, Marlene Sophie, 161n12
Alzheimer's disease, 123
American Sociological Association, 51, 120
American Sociologist, 119
analytic autoethnography, 122–24, 162n24
Andersen, Margaret, 50, 161n9; *Getting Smart about Race* by, 58; on sponsors and mentors, 59
Anderson, Elijah, 156n13
Anderson, Leon, 128; on analytic autoethnography, 122, 123, 124, 162n24; Bochner and Ellis responding to, 125

Annals, 155n12
anthropologists, on autoethnography, 121
Anzaldúa, Gloria, 56
artificial intelligence (AI), 137–38
assignments: personal writing, 138–39; on sociological autobiography, 129, 132, 133–38, 145; student judgment in, 134–35; word limits for, 136
Atkinson, Paul, 124
At the Heart of Work and Family (Hansen and Garey), 57–58
autobiographers, 32
autobiographical pact: Lejeune on, 36; veracity and, 36–38
autobiographical selves, 34; Bjorklund on, 100–101; Smith, Sidonie, and Watson on, 28–31, 90–91; of women and men, 30–31, 151n8
autobiographical sociology, 119–20, 122
autobiographical writing, teaching with, 131–39
autobiographies, 4–5, 27, 28; autobiographical sociology, 119–20, 122; *The Autobiography of Malcolm X*, 3, 87–88; *The Autobiography of W. E. B. Du Bois*, 65; Bjorklund research on, 99–101, 105–6; *Darkwater*, 65; *Dusk of Dawn*, 65; *In the Field*, 65; *Interpreting the Self* on, 97, 99–101; *Participant Observer*, 65, 70; sociological autobiography, 118, 119–20, 122, 129, 131, 132, 133–38, 145; of sociologists, 11, 47–48, 144. See also *Autobiography of a Face*

ABOUT THE AUTHOR

Margaret K. Nelson is the A. Barton Hepburn Professor Emerita of Sociology at Middlebury College. She is the author of many books, including, recently, *Like Family: Narratives of Fictive Kinship* and *Keeping Family Secrets: Shame and Silence in Memoirs from the 1950s*. With Emily K. Abel she has co-authored *Limited Choices: Mable Jones, a Black Children's Nurse in a Northern White Household* and *The Farm & Wilderness Summer Camps: Progressive Ideals in the Twentieth Century*.